Friends for Jannah

Build and Nurture Authentic
Relationships with Islamic Values

SARAH GULFRAZ

Copyright © 2025 Sarah Gulfraz

Sarah Gulfraz has asserted her right to be identified as the author of this Work in accordance with the Copyright, Designs and Patents Act 1988.

All rights reserved.

No portion of this book may be reproduced in any form, stored in a retrieval system, stored in a database, or published/transmitted in any form or by any means, electronic, mechanical, photocopying, recording or otherwise, without prior written permission of the publisher.

Dedication

~ Bismillah ~

May Allah (swt) accept our efforts and grant us success in this life and the next. Ameen.

In dedication to my loving family and all their support.

Contents

1. Introduction — 1
2. Introduction to Friendship in Islam — 4
3. The Prophetic Model of Friendship — 19
4. Types of Friendship in Islamic Tradition — 29
5. Building and Nurturing Friendships — 40
6. Loyalty and Support in Friendship — 53
7. Challenges in Friendships and Their Resolutions — 63
8. Friendship with Allah (SWT) — 73
9. Friendship Ethics in Islam — 82
10. Stories of Friendship from Islamic History — 92
11. Applying Lessons of Friendship in Everyday Life — 100
12. Conclusion — 106

Find Out More — 108

Chapter One

Introduction

Humans are sociable creatures by nature. Regardless of whether a person identifies as extroverted or introverted, there is no denying that social connections are essential to our existence. According to Islam, friendship is one of the divine gifts that help people get over feelings of isolation and loneliness.

The best way to characterise "Islam" is as a comprehensive and all-encompassing code of life that offers detailed and wide-ranging guidelines about every aspect of existence. While the Holy Quran provides a theorised version of these rules, the lives of the Holy Prophet (PBUH) and his family and companions (A.S.) provide the most practical examples of how they are put into practice.

Their mutual belief in Allah (SWT) and duty to support the emerging Muslim community served as the foundation for their friendship. They all experienced their share of hardships and made a special place in history throughout the decades, their influence always felt strong. Moreover, it's crucial to remember that the Holy Prophet's (PBUH) friends and associates were significant in the founding, growth, and propagation of Islam.

Humans have nearly always been gregarious animals who require company. They interacted with one another even when they lived in caves, which facilitated greater bonding and grouping. Islam values friendship and sociability highly. The Quran emphasises the importance of friendship, which is crucial to a person's development and determines the course they'll take in life.

> *Allah (SWT) says, "And hold firmly to the rope of Allah all together, and do not become divided" (Quran 3:103)*

This verse reflects the essence of being together with others by building relationships that promote togetherness, unity, and shared values, such as friendship.

Our friends influence many facets of our lives and play a significant role in our personality development; these friends are an essential and significant element of our social lives. Throughout our lives, we frequently encounter hardships that leave us feeling hopeless and challenges that appear out of nowhere. These challenges can significantly reduce our productivity. Strong bonds with our friends give us the support and fortitude to overcome these difficulties.

Additionally, there will always be someone available to assist you when needed. From a psychological standpoint, these beneficial connections lessen anxiety and the tension that goes along with it. Being surrounded by people who appreciate you fosters emotional stability and contentment.

> *Imam Ali (AS), the Commander of the Faithful, beautifully advises: "Try to have as many as possible true friends, for they are the supplies in joy and the shelters in misfortunes." (Nahjul Balagha)*

This wisdom highlights the importance and need of genuine friendships, emphasising friends as a source of support and comfort in both pleasure and harsh conditions.

The children of Adam (AS) were made to value friendship and companionship, and the wise seek the company of those who support them both here on Earth and in the Hereafter. True friendships are mutually beneficial, and those who accept honourable, devout, and honest companions align themselves with the righteous.

Then there are those who enjoy this world's glitz and glamour and only care about gratifying their whims, lusts, and desires. They befriend criminals and transgressors, harming rather than uplifting one another, and ultimately distancing farther and farther away from Allah (SWT). It's a privilege from Allah (SWT) to have such honourable associates both here on Earth and in the Hereafter.

> *"Close friends, that Day, will be enemies to each other, except for the righteous." (Quran 43:67)*

> *When describing the influence of friends, the Holy Prophet (PBUH) states: "A man follows the religion of his close friend; therefore, let each of you look carefully at whom he takes as a close friend." (Tirmidhi)*

Because friendships have a powerful influence on one's values and behaviour, this hadith serves as a reminder to surround oneself with people who uplift one's spirit and deepen one's faith.

This manual aims to give readers a thorough understanding of the nature of friendship in accordance with Islamic principles through the teachings of the Quran, prophetic examples of bonding with companions, ethical guidelines, and motivational tales from Islamic history. It also emphasises the importance of companionship in Islam and provides doable strategies for creating and preserving deep connections founded on the Islamic values of compassion, loyalty, and support for one another.

Chapter Two

Introduction to Friendship in Islam

Importance of Friendship (Suhbah) in Islam

The Quran gives a lot of attention to human relationships, whether benevolent and empathetic or antagonistic and antagonistic. A relationship between two or more people distinguished by affection, trust, and a good attitude towards the "other" is called friendship and a positive relationship. Friends have a "bond." Making new friends is a happy moment.

In Islam, friendship is highly valued. According to the teachings of the Quran, Muslims are "one brotherhood." A brother is closer than a friend. Therefore, the desire to create a brotherhood transcends friendship. One of the best ways to promote brotherhood is through friendship. Allah (SWT) commands Muslims to assist one another in good deeds and not assist one another in mischief.

The foundation of true friendship is moral and spiritual. We're all aware that Allah (SWT) the Most High created us with a specific purpose and life is a test for all of us. None of us will dispute that we're only here for a brief time and that we will eventually meet Allah (SWT).

Selecting the appropriate companions is crucial for Muslims to uphold their faith. Maintaining the Straight Path requires making friends with morally upright Muslims. On the other side, Muslims should constantly aim to be strong individuals since they are the foundation of a strong community.

> *Allah (SWT) in the Holy Quran says: "On that Day the wrongdoer will bite his hands saying: Oh! Would that I had only taken the pathway alongside the Prophet Oh! Would that I had never chosen so-and-so for my companion. He was the one who led me astray from the admonition, even after it had reached me. Shaitan is ever treacherous to man." (Quran 27:29)*

Allah (SWT) understands the value of having a good friend in one's life. The "choosing of a good friend" is the verse's most significant part. The Holy Quran states that companions or associates tend to mislead a person. Hence, we should treat the remainder with grace and justice and befriend the virtuous instead of the wronged.

Quranic Terms Highlighting the Value of Companionship

The Quran uses various terms to describe friendship, one of which is "Sahib" (plural form: ashāb). Although this term has several meanings, it describes something that goes with another thing, whether an animal or a human. As a result, "Sahib" is more comprehensive than friendship and mostly indicates familiarity and long-term companionship.

For example, the pagans of Makkah had lived alongside Prophet Muhammad (PBUH) and knew him well. Yet, when he presented to them as their Sahib—companion or friend—they rejected Islam.

> "Say, —Shall we invoke besides Allah (SWT) that which can neither benefit us nor harm us, and turn back on our heels after Allah (SWT) has guided us, like someone seduced by the devils and bewildered on the earth, who has companions that invite him to guidance, [saying,] Come to us!'? Say, —Indeed it is the guidance of Allah (SWT) which is [true] guidance, and we have been commanded to submit to the Lord of all the worlds." (Quran 6:71)

Khalil (plural form: akhilla) is another term used for friend in the Quran. This term refers to a personal friend, and the root word "khullah" signifies friendship that has deeply permeated the heart and affection with the utmost purity.

> Referring to this kind of companionship, the Quran says that "on the Day of Judgment there will be people who will regret becoming intimate friends, khalil, with impious people who made them forget Allah (SWT) and His message, rather than having befriended righteous people." (Quran 25:27-28)

It will be too late for them to alter their circumstances, though, once they understand that they have made their true foes into friends and their true friends into enemies.

Intriguingly, Allah (SWT) selects certain individuals to be His khalīl. It's possible to be a khalīl of Allah (SWT). Hazrat Abraham (AS) was honoured when Allah (SWT) made him a friend, and since we're all Hazrat Abraham (AS)'s followers, it's likewise a great honour for all of us. According to Imam Sadiq (a), Hazrat Abraham (AS) never turned down a request from anyone, and he never asked anyone but Allah (SWT), which is why Allah (SWT) picked him as a friend.

> *The Quran says: "Who is better in his faith than the person who submits himself to Allah (SWT) and follows the path of Abraham? And Allah (SWT) chose Abraham as his friend. (Quran 4:125)*

Akh (plural form: Ikhwah) is another noun. The use of this term in the Quran attests to the fact that, despite its literal meaning of brother, it can also denote friend. The literal meaning—biological brother—has expanded to include an acquaintance that belongs to the same tribe, country, religion, or philosophy.

Another term used for friend in the Quran is "Sadiq" which comes from the root sidq, which means truth, and is used to describe a sincere and truthful friend. The following verses from the Quran utilise this phrase, and both times it's used in the singular:

> *"Now we have no intercessors, nor do we have any sympathetic friend. Had there been another turn for us, we would be among the faithful." (Quran 26:100-102)*

Hamīm can also be used as a noun on its own and is frequently translated as "friend" or "a friend who is close, devoted, or considerate." Such usage is found in the verses that follow:

> *"[A]nd no friend will inquire about [the welfare of his] friend, [though they will be placed within each other's sight]. The guilty one will wish he could ransom himself from the punishment of that day at the price of his children, his spouse and his brother, his kin which had sheltered him and all those who are upon the earth, if that might deliver him." (Quran 70:10-14)*

> "Warn them of the Imminent Day when hearts will be at the throats, choking with suppressed agony, [and] the wrongdoers will have no friend, nor any intercessor who might be heard." (Quran 40:18)

Another word for friend in Islam is "Wali," one of the most profound ideas. At its core, Wali represents a reciprocal relationship between two or more individuals who share a common cause, are members of the same party or community, and are led by the same person.

The Quran exquisitely depicts the many facets of friendship, from light-hearted company to profound spiritual ties. According to the Quranic verses above, humans can develop empathetic and constructive connections with one another in various ways and to varying degrees. The Quran emphasises how friendships affect one's beliefs and destiny with terms like Sahib, Khalil, Akh, Sadiq, Hamim, and Wali. According to the Quran, genuine friendship fosters righteousness and draws people nearer to Allah (SWT).

Understanding the Concept of Brotherhood/Sisterhood (Ukhuwwah) in Islam

Brotherhood is a fundamental idea in Islam, highlighted by the Quran as the cornerstone of fostering amicable human connections. According to the Quran, fraternity is a moral and spiritual tie that unites people rather than merely a blood tie. Brotherhood entails respect, affection, and assistance for one another despite disparities in race, ethnicity, and social standing.

Maintaining harmonious relationships (Ukhuwwah) with other humans is a prerequisite for human perfection as Allah's (SWT) servant, while worshipping Allah (SWT) alone (hamlum minallah) is insufficient.

In the Quran, Allah (SWT) says: "The Believers are but a single Brotherhood: so make peace and reconciliation between your two (contending) brothers; and fear Allah, that you may receive Mercy." (Quran 49:10)

"And hold fast, all together, by the Rope which Allah (stretches out for you), and be not divided among yourselves. And remember with gratitude Allah's favor on you; for you were enemies and He joined your hearts in love, so that by His Grace, you became brethren; and you were on the brink of the Pit of Fire, and He saved you from it. Thus does Allah make His Signs clear to you: that you may be guided" (Quran 3:103)

Islamic unity surpasses any distinctions in terms of race, nationality, colour, or language. The beauty of the term "Ukhuwwah" is that it arouses feelings of love and affection in addition to the desire for justice and equality. Because of their profound faith, the early Muslims developed a brotherhood and sisterhood that Allah (SWT) considered one of His bounties.

Brotherhood is encouraged throughout the Muslim Ummah. Our Ibadat, as Muslims, encourages unity. We discover union and camaraderie when we stand shoulder to shoulder in our collective prayers. When Muslims gather from all over the world to perform the Hajj, when we fast together during the month of Ramadan, or when we give to the poor and needy through our Zakat and Sadaqar, we not only worship Allah (SWT) but also learn about and deepen the ties that bind us to one another. All other Islamic laws and regulations aim to strengthen and advance a fraternal and cohesive Muslim community.

> *The Holy Prophet (PBUH) said: "A Muslim is a brother to another Muslim; he does not oppress him, does not disappoint him, and does not hand him over (to the enemy)." (Bukhari & Muslim)*

The fact that a Muslim is a brother to another Muslim means that all Muslims are brothers in faith, which means that they must love and support one another; He does not oppress him, which forbids a Muslim from physically, mentally, or materially oppressing his brother; He does not disappoint him, which forbids a Muslim from failing his brother, which means not turning him over to the enemy or harming him; and He refrains from giving him over (to the enemy).

Because it teaches mutual respect, support, and the defence of others in the Islamic society, this hadith offers Muslims great moral advice when interacting with other Muslims. Basically, there are three types of brotherhood (Ukhuwwah) that were formed in Islam: a. Ukhuwwah Islamiyah, b. Ukhuwwah Basyariyah, and c. Ukhuwwah Wathaniyah.

Ukhuwwah Islamiyah

Ukhuwwah Islamiyah indicates that, in Islam, all people who share the same faith—regardless of their origins, language, or ethnicity—are brothers. Every Muslim has a duty to treat one another with respect and support each other like real brothers.

Prophet Muhammad (PBUH) emphasised that a person's level of social responsiveness towards others is a good indicator of how strong their faith is. People who are religious are uncomfortable with other people's suffering, which makes them want to support and assist them.

> *"A Muslim is a brother to another, it is not permissible to hurt each other or let others be hurt. Whoever covers the needs of his brother, Allah will also cover his needs, and whoever wants to overcome the difficulties of a*

> *Muslim, Allah will overcome his difficulties later on the Day of Judgment, and whoever conceals the 'ugliness of a Muslim, then Allah will also hide the 'ugliness of his later in life Judgment Day." (Sahih Bukhari)*

In another place Prophet Muhammad (PBUH) mentioned that the brotherhood of religion is like a single body; when one part of it is ill, the entire body suffers. It goes without saying that a nice condition of peace will result if this idea is truly applied in Muslim culture. In a hadith, the Prophet Muhammad disclosed this:

> *"The brotherhood of the believers in establishing love and affection between them is like one body. When a part of the body hurts, the pain spreads to all the other members of the body, so that one cannot sleep and feels hot." (Muttafaqun 'Alaih)*

It's now obvious that in Islam, there is synergism between Muslims, wherein one must cooperate by showing affection for one another and supporting one another in overcoming obstacles for the benefit of all.

Ukhuwwah Basyariyah

Human fraternity is known as Ukhuwwah Basyariyah. This indicates that the realisation that people are Allah's (SWT) most ideal creation awakens brotherhood. Since this life is Allah's (SWT) most flawless creation, there is no need for anyone to feel obligated or accountable for enjoying it. This kind of awareness is necessary, particularly if we live in a pluralistic environment. Only in a pluralistic culture can Ukhuwwah Basyariyah be achieved if everyone is acutely conscious of their status as social creatures whose existence and involvement depend on others.

The idea that humans are the best creation of Allah (SWT), as stated in the letter at-Tin as "ahsani taqwim," fosters a sense of fraternity among people.

> In the Quran, it's stated that: *"We have certainly created man in the best of stature." (Quran 95:4)*

This verse emphasises the honour and perfection in which human beings have been created, both physically and spiritually.

As a result, people are naturally inspired to make a commitment to do the best (al-Ashlah) and the good (al-saleh) things in their lives. Because the goal of Islamic law is to establish continuity (at-Tawazun) in life, a Muslim must constantly refrain from acts that produce social breakdown or conflict.

Therefore, the success of Ukhuwwah Basyariyah depends on whether or not each person can live their best and accomplish good deeds. Consequently, equality is "the enabling element for the emergence of brotherhood in a broad or limited sense." The primary element before the emergence of true brotherhood is equality of taste and affection, which ultimately causes a person to empathise with his brother's suffering, extend an offer before being asked, and serve him with respect.

Ukhuwwah Wathaniyah

This implies that all people who reside in the same nation are inherently brothers (Ukhuwwah Wathaniyah). Ukhuwwah Wathaniyah can be understood as brothers and sisters in the same nation, irrespective of ethnicity, language, culture, or religion, since the word "wathaniyah" is derived from the word "wathan" and means homeland, country, or place of birth.

Every ummah from every generation that has ever been on Earth has its unique Qiblah in Islam. This implies that it's impossible to avoid pluralism. As a result, the state allows its inhabitants to freely select and choose the religion that best suits their convictions. This conveys the idea that it's impossible to avoid religious, cultural, and ethnic variety.

It should be highlighted, nevertheless, that religious variety is susceptible to conflict since, in the sociologist's opinion, and the things that make conflict worse are basic ideological disagreements brought on by disapproval of other groups' beliefs.

Religion can indeed bring people together, bond them together, and maintain them, but it can also be a force that drives them apart and even destroys them. If followers of each religion can create and cultivate an ethic of interreligious peace, tolerance will be achieved. The purpose of religion's transmission was to give individuals a path for seeking truth in various ways, not to divide or condemn.

> *In the Quran, it is said that: "Say (O you believers); "We believe in Allah and what was revealed to us, and what was revealed to Abraham, Isma'il, Ishaq, Ya'kub and their descendants, and what was given to Musa and Isa and what was given to the prophets from their Lord. We do not discriminate between any of them and we only submit to Him." (Quran 2:136)*

It's evident that religious pluralism is an unchangeable sunnatullah, and the Quran directly legalises its existence. Accordingly, religious people believe that differences in beliefs shouldn't stand in the way of doing good deeds and the best in humanity; instead, they should support one another and not harbour animosity towards one another according to Islamic teachings.

> "*Allah does not forbid you to do well and do justice to those who do not fight because of religion and do not expel you from your country. Verily, Allah loves those who act justly.*" (Quran 60:8)

As long as they don't harbour animosity towards others in the name of their faith, as the Quran explains, Muslims are free to treat everyone with kindness, justice, and friendship. As His word describes, the Quran actually forbids Muslims from mistreating someone simply because it's motivated by enmity.

> "*O you who believe, be those who always uphold (the truth) for Allah, witness fairly. And don't let your hatred of a people encourage you to act unjustly. Be fair, because fairness is closer to piety. And fear Allah, Verily Allah is Aware of what you do.*" (Quran 5:8)

Muslims are commanded to constantly have cordial relationships with followers of other religions, according to the teachings mentioned above. Based on the aforementioned explanations, it can be inferred that if all religious followers are mature enough to comprehend their beliefs, those beliefs will promote peace and brotherhood because all religions teach that respect and love for one another must be realised in one's life.

Islamic brotherhood aims to bring Muslims together in harmony, peace, and solidarity. As brothers or sisters, Muslims are supposed to help one another through good times and bad. They must be prepared to help, shield, and encourage one another. Muslims should coexist peacefully if they love, respect, and understand one another.

Islam's idea of brotherhood upholds the equality of all Muslims in society and before the law. No Muslim must be subjected to unjust treatment or discrimination. In conclusion, the idea of "Muslim brotherhood" highlights the value of close, loving, and respectful bonds amongst human beings. Islamic teachings, which strongly emphasise the value of solidarity and unity among its adherents, include this as a fundamental component.

Virtues and Characteristics of a Good Friend (Sahib)

As Islam places a high value on being sociable, peaceful and respectful to others and treating them fairly.

> *The Holy Quran states that: "And of two parties of believers fall to fighting, then make peace between them...make peace between them justly and act equitably. Lo! Allah Loveth the equitable." (Quran 49:9)*

This Quranic verse makes it very evident how much Allah (SWT) values preserving justice, equity, and peace on His lands, and friendships are among the most direct and efficient means of doing this. Conflicts are less likely to occur when people have strong relationships with one another, which ultimately pleases Allah (SWT). Muslims must therefore be close good friends since it's one way to appease the Creator. What does good friend mean? Which type of qualities does a good friend possess? Let's look in detail.

Qualities of a Righteous Companion according to Islamic Principles

In Islam, a good friend helps you become closer to Allah (SWT), His Prophet (PBUH), and His faith. A Muslim believes that this world and its joys are fleeting and that the only way to be satisfied or absolved truly is to strive for Allah's (SWT) will and pleasure, this is a road in which a good companion can be helpful.

The righteous friend himself is a virtuous person who obeys Allah (SWT), follows religious teachings, is eager to please Allah (SWT), hastens to perform all good deeds out of faith, turns away from all evil deeds has fear of Allah (SWT), respects the Sunnah and those who follow it, opposes (the enemies of Allah SWT) for Allah's (SWT) sake, dislikes sin, is pure-hearted and virtuous, is not boastful, and has no envy or rancour in his heart. When you forget to remember your creator, the virtuous friend reminds you of Him; he supports and joins you in remembering your creator.

> *"The example of a good companion in comparison with a bad one, is like that of the musk seller and the blacksmith's bellows (or furnace); from the first you would either buy musk or enjoy its good smell while the bellows would either burn your clothes or your house, or you get a bad nasty smell thereof." (Sahih Bukhari)*

The calibre of the people we spend time with helps us create a positive future. If we don't pick our partners wisely, we may find ourselves on a risky path and find it more difficult to leave that toxic atmosphere. We should choose our friends carefully and ensure that they come from a group of people who uphold morality and condemn immorality.

> *"A man is upon the religion of his best friend, so let one of you look at whom he befriends." (Abu Dawud)*

A few characteristics of a good friend are listed below:

Select a friend with strong character: A person with good character can manage his anger and avoid getting overly excited when he wants something. Be friends with someone who will encourage you to accomplish something good while opposing you from doing something bad.

Prefer those who possess intelligence: Being friends with someone who isn't intelligent won't benefit you in any way and will probably result in alienation and loneliness. "How often an ignorant man has destroyed a forgiving man who has befriended him," stated Imam Ali (AS).

They shouldn't be greedy: It is human nature for people to unconsciously adopt the characteristics of those they devote time with. Thus, spending time with a greedy person will make you greedier, whereas spending time with an empathetic friend will make you more generous.

They ought to be devout: Avoid hanging around with someone who consistently commits serious transgressions and has no fear of Allah (SWT), since their behaviour towards you will fluctuate based on his circumstances and luck.

> *"...And Do not follow him whose mind We have caused to be neglectful of remembrance of Us and who follows his passions, and whose ways are ever in neglect." (Quran 18:28)*

They ought to tell the truth: Dishonest people cause great pain and suffering to their friends and family and undermine the bonds of trust that support society.

> *"It is obligatory for you to tell the truth, for truth leads to virtue and virtue leads to paradise." (Sahih Muslim)*

Moreover, instead of feeling jealous of his brothers for the blessings he observes in their lives, the virtuous friend rejoices in them and gives thanks to Allah (SWT) for all the blessings he sees in them, just as he would give thanks to Allah (SWT) for his own blessings. A good friend treats his brothers with dignity, integrity, and sincerity.

> *Abu Saalih said: "The believer deals with you honourably, and guides you to what is best for you in religious and worldly terms, whereas the hypocrite deals with you through flattery and encourages you to do that which you desire. The fortunate one whom Allah protects is the one who differentiates between the two." (Aadaab as-Suhbah)*

When things get tough, the good friend supports his brothers just as he does when things are easy; he doesn't act any differently towards them in either situation. By doing good deeds for his brothers, ignoring any offence they may have caused him, and looking for justifications, he attempts to win their affection.

In summary, a righteous friend is someone who supports you in doing all that is right, has good morals, forbids wrongdoing, and upholds the rights of friendship both in your presence and absence while paying careful attention to both your words and deeds, all for Allah's (SWT) sake and in the hope of receiving reward from Him.

Chapter Three

The Prophetic Model of Friendship

Prophetic Examples of Friendship

When surrounded by his closest friends and companions, the Prophet (PBUH) consistently provided the best illustration of what a true friend is. It was evident that the Prophet (PBUH) treated his companions well. Prophet Muhammad (PBUH) showed people kindness in a variety of ways in his life. Given that we Muslims are well aware that the Prophet Muhammad (PBUH) possessed a level of proficiency in human interaction and handling that is far higher than that of any other person, this isn't surprising. Allah (SWT) says:

> "And you (Oh Muhammad) are of excellent moral character." (Quran 68:4)

In the eyes of his friends, the Prophet (PBUH) was always observed smiling.

> Ibn Jaz is narrated to have said: "I have not seen anyone who smiled more than the Messenger of Allah"

> *"Allah's Messenger (PBUH) never refused me permission to see him since I embraced Islam and never looked at me but with a smile." (Sahih Muslim)*

> *"Every good is charity. Indeed, among the good is to meet your brother with a smiling face and to pour what is left in your bucket into the vessel of your brother." (Tirmidhi)*

The Holy Prophet (PBUH) consistently appealed to his friends' and companions' needs. At times, the Prophet (PBUH) would inspire people to do good deeds by telling them of the enormous benefits they would receive in exchange, whether they were rewards of this world or the next, even though he would never compromise his duty to preserve the religion of Allah (SWT).

For instance, the Prophet (PBUH) advised his fellows that they would win the affection of Allah (SWT) and humanity if they gave up worldly pursuits.

The Prophet Muhammad (PBUH) had a reputation for being patient and never losing his temper over trivial issues. According to Anas Bin Malik, who served the Prophet (PBUH) for more than a decade, the Prophet (PBUH) never once expressed disapproval of him.

> *Anas Bin Malik stated: "I served the Prophet (PBUH) at Medina for ten years. I was a boy. Every work I did was not according to the desire of my master, but he never said to me: Fie, nor did he say to me: Why did you do this? Or why did you not do this?" (Sunah Abi Dawud)*

The Prophet (PBUH) favoured making each other's lives easy.

> *"He who alleviates the suffering of a brother out of the sufferings of the world, Allah would alleviate his suffering from the sufferings of the Day of Resurrection, and he who finds relief for one who is hard-pressed, Allah would make things easy for him in the Hereafter..."*
> *(Sahih Muslim)*

Others respected the Companions because the Messenger of Allah (PBUH) often commended them and praised their positive qualities. The way the Messenger of Allah (PBUH) interacted with his Companions showed that he loved each of them; his love for each Companion was distinct from his love for the others. The Prophet Muhammad (PBUH) joked with his companions and was always kind to them.

> *For example, the Holy Prophet (PBUH) appreciated one of the Companions despite the fact that he did not look good. One day, when he was peddling his wares, the Holy Prophet approached him from behind and hugged him. "Leave me alone," the man pleaded, unable to see who was clutching him. "Who are you?" When the man looked around, he recognised that it was Holy Prophet. The Messenger of Allah responded to this by humorously asking, "Who will buy a slave?" "Oh Messenger of Allah, you'll not get much for me," the guy retorted. Next, the Prophet Muhammad stated, "But in Allah's (SWT) eyes, you are valuable," or "But in Allah's (SWT) eyes, you are not cheap." He told him the truth, but he was making a joke. According to Abu Hurayrah, the Messenger of Allah stated, "I only speak the truth." A few of his companions remarked, "But you make fun of us?" "I only say the truth," the Messenger of Allah retorted. (Ahmed)*

This is how we discovered what Allah (SWT), and His Messenger (PBUH) had taught us about friendship—how to approach it for Allah's (SWT) sake, the benefits of excellent company, and some lovely ways to maintain friendships that are rooted in faith.

Stories of Friendship from the Life of Prophet Muhammad (PBUH)

When the Prophet (PBUH) was in the Cave of Hira with his closest friend and companion Abu Bakr al-Siddiq (RA), he gave us the clearest illustration of a true friend. Abu Bakr Siddiq (RA) was Prophet Muhammad's (PBUH) best friend and companion. Muslims throughout the world are still motivated by his life and legacy. Abu Bakr (RA), the first man to convert to Islam, supported the Prophet (PBUH) no matter what. In the early days of Islam, his steadfast support was crucial.

They were sheltering in a Hira cave when murderous assailants were just centimetres away. Who wouldn't feel anxious and in a panic? Who wouldn't be depressed? Quite literally, the adversary will discover you and take you into custody. But to reassure him, the Prophet (PBUH) said: 'Do not grieve (and) feel sorrow...'

Abu Bakr (RA) and Prophet Muhammad (PBUH) had one of the strongest friendships in history. Only a good friend wants to help their friend overcome their misery since they can't handle it themselves. That is a crucial aspect of friendship. You try to support, uplift, and provide your friend honest counsel when they are at their lowest or in a trying circumstance. The issue is that while the Prophet (PBUH) didn't stop there, most people do.

> *Rather, he ended by saying: ... "Surely, Allah is with us."*
> *(Quran 9:40)*

He linked Allah (SWT) to his friend. He reminded him that his faith and dependence on Allah (SWT) were crucial. A friend should take care of you, but it's just as important—if not more so—that they take good care of you. He is concerned enough to bring Allah (SWT) to your attention. A good friend is more concerned about your future than your present; he will preach to you, try to draw you closer to Him, and guide you on the correct path.

At the same time during the most trying circumstances, Abu Bakr (RA) always supported the Prophet (PBUH). Abu Bakr (RA) remained steadfast in supporting the Prophet (PBUH) and his adherents when the Quraish elders in Makkah turned against them.

Despite being persecuted alongside Muslims, he never abandoned the Prophet (PBUH). The Quran emphasises the strong relationship between Prophet Muhammad (PBUH) and Abu Bakr (RA) by mentioning their stay at the Cave of Thawr during the journey from Makkah to Madinah. The passage says:

> *"It does not matter if you believers do not support him, for Allah did in fact support him when the disbelievers drove him out of Makkah and he was only one of two. While they both were in the cave, he reassured his companion, 'Do not worry; Allah is certainly with us."*
> *(Quran 9:40)*

By referring to Abu Bakr (RA) as the Prophet's (PBUH) "companionship," this verse recognises their close relationship. Allah's (SWT) comfort and protection throughout this time demonstrate that He liked and supported their friendship and shows His approval of it.

Guidance on Choosing Positive Influences (Suhbah Salihah)

Being able to look up to and appreciate someone might be crucial to our development and achievement. Everyone needs someone they can admire, even if that person is just an example of dealing with challenging situations. It's not enough to have someone we aspire to be like; we also need someone we respect, trust, and look up to for leadership. The people in our lives teach us a lot, therefore it's critical that they have a positive impact on us.

> *"And keep yourself patient [by being] with those who call upon their Lord in the morning and the evening, seeking His countenance. And let not your eyes pass beyond them, desiring adornments of the worldly life. And do not obey one whose heart we have made heedless of Our remembrance and who follows his desire and whose affair is [ever] in neglect." (Quran 18:28)*

This verse emphasises staying in the company of righteous and sincere individuals rather than those who are heedless of Allah (SWT).

When we surround ourselves with encouraging and positive friends, our confidence in ourselves and our skills rises. Additionally, having someone who guides us with optimism makes us stronger emotionally and psychologically, helping us overcome any obstacles that may arise.

When we see the positive aspects of both people and circumstances, we have a much better perspective on life. Instead of immediately adopting an opposing position, we can develop more advantageous alternatives for all parties. Additionally, we acquire valuable insights, gain new abilities, and form relationships that we would not have otherwise had if we had not experienced such a significant impact on our lives. All things considered, being a positive influence can truly broaden our perspectives and enhance our general well-being.

Make the decision to associate with people who will hold you to a high standard. People who know and care about you'll want you to succeed. They are well aware of your abilities, intelligence, and talent. They won't allow you to fall short of your full potential since they believe in you. Someone in your close circle is most likely not looking out for your best interests if they don't hold you to high expectations or expect much of you. That's why positive influences matter in life.

> *The Prophet (PBUH) also said: "The example of a good companion and a bad companion is like that of the seller of musk and the one who blows the bellows (blacksmith). The seller of musk will either give you some as a gift, or you will buy some from him, or at least you will smell its fragrance. As for the one who blows the bellows, he will either burn your clothes or you will get an offensive smell from him." (Sahih Bukhari & Sahih Muslim)*

Criteria For Selecting Friends Who Uphold Islamic values

Making good and pious friends is very important in Islam since the people we spend time with can greatly influence our beliefs, behaviour, and deeds. Although most of us will have many friends throughout our lives, only a few will become close friends. It's difficult to find good friends, and it's even more difficult to keep up solid communities and friendships.

Friends are like blossoms. You want to keep some of them close at hand since they smell and look nice. Some are aesthetically pleasing even though they have no scent at all. Others have thorns that, if not handled carefully, can cause pain. Some flowers need considerable care but may bring a lot of goodness into your life, while others are simple to maintain and continue to bloom year after year with little work. You'll always select the finest bouquet to adorn your house. Similarly, we should constantly choose the greatest friends who will help us and serve as a reminder of Allah (SWT).

We must always keep the Akhirah in mind when we make decisions in life. Without further ado, let's talk about the characteristics we ought to consider when selecting friends:

We must pick a friend who respects the teachings of Allah (SWT) and the Prophet Muhammad (PBUH) and adheres to Islam. Additionally, we should avoid those who are rude and don't care about Islam or what Allah (SWT) likes or dislikes because they'll undoubtedly harm us. If the companion drowns us in our misdeeds and makes us unpopular with Allah (SWT), then there is no good. Those who follow wicked paths have rotten motivations behind their activities based on deviation and poor leadership.

Select someone who improves your Imaan. A genuine friend is someone who makes you think about Allah (SWT) and with whom you feel at ease doing deen. Just having a casual talk with them can make you feel better. A cool conversation with a good friend can elevate your spirits and improve your Imaan, even if you're having trouble with your religion or are carrying a heavy load of guilt.

Before selecting a friend, ensure they are truthful people and not dishonest. The foundation of any successful and healthy relationship is honesty and trust. You shouldn't hang out with a friend who isn't always honest with you. You should surround yourself with individuals who will express their honest thoughts on matters without regard for your response. You'll save a lot of money if you choose honest friends.

Thus, it's crucial to choose carefully who we want to be friends with and whom we should avoid. There have been a lot of talks about this and the significance of picking a good friend. This problem has also received particular attention from the Infallible Imams (AS).

A lovely phrase from Imam Sajjad (AS), about the splendour of the worshippers, has been cited in this regard and explains some of the requirements for selecting a friend. The book Usul al-Kafi recounts what Imam Sajjad (AS) said to his esteemed son, Imam Baqir (AS): He said avoid becoming five people's friend, companion, or interlocutor who:

- Steer clear of a liar's company because he mimics a mirage that deceives you by appearing far away from you and then appearing close again.

- Avoid being around a fool because, despite his best efforts to help you, he will hurt you because of his ignorance.

- A stingy individual will take away your wealth when you most need him, so stay away from him.

- A transgressor would betray you for less than a meal, so stay away from his company.

Stay away from people who have severed their family ties because I have discovered that they are far from Allah's (SWT) kindness in three different places in the Holy Quran.

> *Allah (SWT) has said: "But if you held command, you were sure to make mischief in the land and cut off the ties of kinship! Those it is whom Allah has cursed so He has made them deaf and blinded their eyes." (Quran 47:22-23)*

Thus, it's our duty as Muslims to be good friends and pick our friends carefully. We can create solid and meaningful connections that enhance our lives and help us become better Muslims and people by adhering to the Quran's important teachings and the Sunnah about seeking out uplifting and encouraging friendships.

Identifying Negative Friendships According to Islamic Teachings

Similar to a good or quality friendship, several factors can help identify the traits of a bad friendship. The first and most important of these traits—hypocrisy—has been exposed by Allah (SWT) Himself. People who pretend to be friends but lie, betray, backbite, and desert others when they are in need are known as hypocrites.

> *"The hypocrites, both men and women, precede one from another. They enjoin the wrong, and they forbid the right, and they withhold their hands (from spending for the cause of Allah). They forget Allah, so He hath forgotten them. Lo! The hypocrites, they are the transgressors."* (Quran 9:67)

The Quran gives believers advice by pointing out warning indicators, such as the need to avoid becoming friends with hypocrites because they would not only perish in hellfire themselves but will probably drag you down with them. This is a challenging duty because no one fully discloses themselves to others, making it impossible to determine an apparent acquaintance's true character and friendliness.

Choosing friends and companions carefully is crucial for any Muslim who wishes to preserve and defend his faith. According to Islam, a good friend encourages you to remember Allah (SWT) and walk in His way. A good friend's words broaden your understanding, and his deeds inspire you to walk in the right route both here on Earth and in the next.

Chapter Four

Types of Friendship in Islamic Tradition

Importance of Productive Relationships in Islam

Proactive relationships are interpersonal connections that increase productivity and help you succeed in all facets of life. You can develop these kinds of ties in your neighbourhood, workplace, friends, and family.

In the future, Allah (SWT) will reward you for establishing healthy connections, including treating everyone you encounter with kindness. This ought to be our first goal while attempting to establish fruitful connections. In Islam, establishing wholesome connections is important for the sake of Allah (SWT), and we're taught in our faith to cultivate solid and wholesome relationships based on respect, kindness, and compassion for others.

We frequently encounter difficulties that seem to appear out of nowhere and sufferings that leave us feeling hopeless. These problems can significantly reduce our productivity. Proactive partnerships provide the support and resilience we need to overcome these challenges.

Additionally, because of how you treat people, you'll always have someone to lend you a helping hand when you need it, whether it be a friend, relative, or coworker. Each of them will be more than pleased to assist. From a psychological standpoint, healthy relationships lessen worry and the stress that goes along with it. Because you'll be surrounded by people who like you, they also foster emotional stability and contentment.

> *"And do good; indeed, Allah loves the doers of good"* (Quran 2:195)

In addition, we're adhering to the Sunnah of our Prophet (PBUH), who was the pinnacle of human achievement and productivity. His amazing treatment of his friends, wives, kids, and the entire Muslim community is something we read and hear about all the time. Why not build fruitful connections the way he did?

> *"The most perfect believer in respect of faith is he who is best of them in manners." (Abu Dawud)*

Understanding Various Forms of Friendship

Connecting with others helps us overcome feelings of loneliness by giving us a sense of love and belonging. In actuality, a hierarchy of needs states that in addition to necessities like food, drink, and safety, we also need to fill the wants of love and belonging to survive. As a result, maintaining our tight relationships must be our top priority.

As previously stressed, human connections can range from very dear to casually maintained ties with other individuals. But because they have so many positive effects on physical and mental health, they are all essential to humans. The concept of interconnectivity, which holds that we're all related, is born out of connections with other people.

The Quran concludes with a brief chapter titled "Small Kindnesses" (Al-Ma'un). In it, Allah (SWT) describes a person who has lost his faith because he no longer feels connected to others.

> *"Have you ever seen a human being who contradicts the faith in God and His Judgment? That is the person who pushes the orphan aside and does not promote feeding the poor. Woe, then, unto those who pray, but their hearts and minds are remote from the essence of their prayers, those who appear to pray, but refuse to share the necessities of life with others." (Quran 107:1-7)*

Believing in and worshipping Allah (SWT) isn't enough to succeed in Islam. The test of one's faith would only be half of it. How we interact with other people is the other half test. The blessings that Allah (SWT) bestows upon us are so numerous that it would be impossible to list them all. Furthermore, we cannot make up for all the blessings He has bestowed us. Our relationships with our families, including our parents, siblings, coworkers, students, friends, and Islamic brothers and sisters, are among those blessings.

After all, without the interruption of other people who try to take up our time, energy, and money, it's much simpler to pray, fast, and reflect. However, according to Sharia, the Islamic way of life, we can only genuinely connect with our Creator when serving others. Allah (SWT) loves those who try to treat others with kindness and justice. On the other hand, even if someone fasts tirelessly, prays fervently, or ponders every day, they are a zero if they disregard their obligations to their parents, kids, neighbours, and society at large.

Without a doubt, Islam teaches us the need of having compassion for all of Allah's (SWT) creation. The Prophet Muhammad (PBUH) urged believers to maintain friendships and familial ties, emphasising the need of solid human connections.

> *"Show mercy towards those on earth; the One in heaven will certainly show mercy towards you." (Abu Dawud)*

He emphasised that sustaining positive relationships with family, friends, and the community fosters love, harmony, and a sense of belonging. No matter how big or small, deeds of kindness deepen these ties and promote societal harmony. Islam urges its adherents to be concerned about their neighbours, help those in need, and develop genuine friendships. We fulfil a social obligation and become closer to Allah (SWT) by cultivating meaningful connections.

Importance of Family Ties

Islam places a high importance on family preservation. Interestingly, the Arabic term for family "Usra" is formed from meanings that signify protection, unity, and cohesiveness. Through the Quranic verses and the Seerah of our beloved Prophet (PBUH) Muslims are regularly encouraged to maintain ties within their blood relations for the same reason.

One of the most important forms of ibadat, or worship, that Allah (SWT) accepts is family bonds, or Silatur-Rahim. Silat means "ties through affection and kindness." Anybody who is related by blood to their parents, siblings, uncles, aunts, grandparents, or by marriage is considered a Rahim. It also comes from the name of Allah's (SWT) unique attribute, Ar-Rahman, which means "The Compassionate One." Silatur-Rahim, then, refers to treating family and relatives with kindness and maintaining positive relationships with them. This even applies to relatives who are not Muslims.

> *"The word 'ar-rahm (womb) derives its name from Ar-Rahman (one of the names of Allah) and Allah said: 'I will keep good relation with the one who will keep good relation with you, (womb, kith and kin) and sever the relation with him who will sever the relation with you.'"*
> *(Sahih al-Bukhari)*

For believers who devote their time and energy to fortifying their familial bonds, there are intangible benefits. Numerous allusions to the Quran and Sunnah encourage us to continue the custom of keeping positive relationships with family members and believing that our efforts will be appreciated.

> *Ibn 'Umar narrated, the Prophet (PBUH) said: "Nothing that a man spends on himself and his family, anticipating a reward from Allah, will fail to be rewarded by Allah Almighty. He should begin with those whose support is his responsibility. If there is something left over, he should spend it on his next nearest relative and then the next nearest. (Al-Adab Al-Mufrad)*

Given that family relationships are Allah's (SWT) most cherished act, their great significance is evident. Similarly, breaking off family ties is a severe sin. Family, which is based on love, trust, and steadfast support, is the first and most durable type of friendship. Islam reinforces the idea that family isn't just a duty but also a treasured friendship by teaching that upholding family ties is an act of worship. We discover the solace of family and the delight of genuine companionship in fostering these ties.

Siblings as Friends

Siblings form close friendships with each other. It's because they spent so much time together during their formative years, which compelled them to develop a close relationship. Our relationships change as we age and may be separated by distance, but our siblings were our dearest friends for many of us. Some people's relationships deteriorate, or even worse yet, many others re-establish and forge closer bonds.

Why do re-establishing sibling connections provide solace to many brothers and sisters? They have things in common that no one can replicate, like their shared DNA and bloodlines, their shared childhood memories (playtime, everyday life, travel, friends) and the understanding that a sibling is the sole living link to their parents. Many people find it reassuring to know that someone knows them better than anybody else as they enter the sensitive and perhaps difficult stages of ageing.

It's common for siblings to quarrel, argue, and run around and play together. This is a necessary aspect of maturing that we rarely consider. However, it's unique and fulfilling to have someone, or a number of individuals, at your side as you navigate childhood!

We often take our siblings for granted because our relationships are tested throughout life by various hardships and emotions. Our siblings are rarely regarded as blessings from Allah (SWT), and we're unaware that we can receive "barakah" from them. However, every sibling presents a chance for us to do nice deeds and receive rewards.

There are moments in life when you encounter challenges and adversity. Our thoughts become distracted by what we're currently seeing, and it may seem that good times had never existed. Siblings are wonderful because they serve as a conduit to the blessings of our early years. When you're a youngster, you're carefree, comfortable, innocent, and vibrant. It's good to be reminded of this since it makes you feel renewed and encourages you to have a more thankful and optimistic outlook.

You may believe your relationship with your siblings isn't good after arguing with them. In most cases, Allah (SWT) has blessed people with siblings and a lifelong friend; however, this may be the case in other cases. Until the day comes for you to revert back to Him (SWT), this relationship will endure. You can always talk to your siblings about your thoughts, emotions, and worries. Maintaining the bonds of kinship is the main benefit of this friendship, thus you should always strive to keep it strong.

Spouses as Friends

Each partner presents the other with gifts of common kindness, sincerity, empathy, respect, and trust. Throughout the marriage, the foundation of friendship improves marital happiness. Your success in marriage is built on that friendship. Both spouses ought to consider their life mate to be a genuine friend. Your partner ought to be a friend who supports you during both good and difficult times. Your partner needs to be a friend who understands your aspirations, concerns, and goals. It's critical to know that the foundation of your connection is true friendship.

It's like standing in wet cement when spouses have a strong friendship. It gets harder to get out the longer you stay in it. Additionally, their footprint will always remain even if they are no longer with each other. For Allah's (SWT) sake, a husband and wife ought to be considered best buddies. And that relationship transcends worldly requirements; both support one another in doing good activities that please Allah (SWT). In marriage, friendship needs to be cultivated.

Husband and wife both are Sirat-ul-Mustaqeem Companions.

> *"O you who believe! Ward off yourselves and your families against a Fire (Hell) whose fuel is men and stones..."*
> *(Quran 66:6)*

A good friend wants to help his partner develop as a good person; husbands would plan to watch the kids so their wives could go to class or study the Quran; similarly, a wife could reluctantly plan the family calendar so her husband can spend time with helpful brothers or do good deeds. Moreover, stay prepared for variances in viewpoints, preferences, and even sleeping patterns. Respect and accept each other's differences.

> *"A believer must not hate (his wife) believing woman; if he dislikes one of her characteristics, he will be pleased with another." (Sahih Muslim)*

Remembering to put Allah's (SWT) pleasure first is perhaps the most crucial element in a successful and long-lasting marriage. Everything else falls into place in accordance with His (SWT) will when we faithfully maintain that as our main focus in every work we complete. It's important for spouses to come together, seek Allah's (SWT) blessings by spending time in charity, reading the Quran together, and praying together and by staying together as a long-lasting companion.

Islamic Etiquettes in Interpersonal Relationships

Muslims' daily interactions and interactions with one another are greatly influenced by Islamic etiquettes. What are they? In addition to providing us with detailed instructions for leading a successful and disciplined life, Islam has also taught us how to conduct ourselves with dignity and grace.

Islamic etiquettes and manners are an intrinsic and fundamental element of faith, not anything distinct or foreign. Upholding this facet of our faith makes us likeable to Allah (SWT), our Creator, and His creations. We've learnt manners and etiquette for every situation from our beloved Prophet (PBUH). As Muslims, we must try to learn from the teachings of the Prophet (PBUH) since he is our role model.

> *"It is out of Allah's mercy that you O Prophet have been lenient with them. Had you been cruel or hard-hearted, they would have certainly abandoned you. So pardon them, ask Allah's forgiveness for them, and consult with them in conducting matters. Once you make a decision, put your trust in Allah. Surely Allah loves those who trust in Him." (Quran 3:159)*

Islamic etiquette and good manners teach us how to live in accordance with Islamic teachings and the Sunnah. They refer to lessons that educate us on how to live and behave well when interacting with other people. Let's examine them.

Guidelines for Respectful Interactions with Others

We're inherently engaged in the process of socialisation, or engaging with other people, since we're social creatures with a social spirit. It's also possible that we need to interact with other people to survive. By following the Quran's teachings on manners, we improve interpersonal relationships and create a community that upholds one another, fortifies ties, and creates a calm and tranquil atmosphere for all of its members.

As a manual for living, the Quran offers precise instructions on how to behave in social situations. This lesson stresses respect for others, abstaining from destructive behaviour, and engaging in a kind and courteous manner.

First and foremost, "Adab" is crucial; in Islamic interpersonal relationships, this Islamic etiquette of excellent manners and character is highly valued. Adab is essential to communication because it calls for people to treat one another with deference and consideration while adhering to the Islamic code of ethics and behaviour. Adab is an act of worship towards Allah (SWT) and reflects the goodness of one's character as a Muslim. It represents noble characteristics through honourable words and actions. Additionally, Adab's importance is seen in a variety of communication techniques, such as the dissemination of Islamic teachings, or dakwah, which emphasise "enjoining good and forbidding evil."

It's crucial to follow practical Adab when communicating with others. The below hadith emphasises the propriety of refraining from whispering in private since it could cause third-person sentiments of loneliness or exclusion.

> *The Prophet (PBUH) emphasises the importance of not whispering to others when they are around. He said, "If you are three people, then two should not engage in a private conversation, leaving the third person out, as this could make the third person sad." (Sahih Muslim)*

Moreover, adopting traits like kindness, civility, and the use of good deeds improves communication efficacy and is consistent with the Prophet Muhammad's (PBUH) example of successful communication techniques. The Prophet Muhammad's (PBUH) Interpersonal Communication Model includes verbal and nonverbal communication, rich implications, fluency, parables, voice inflection, message content, comprehending the communicant's circumstances, and refraining from discriminating.

Another element is honesty, which is a key component of Islamic values and attitudes and crucial in interpersonal interactions.

> *"O you who have believed, fear Allah and be with those who are true" (Quran 9:119)*

This exhorts believers to always be truthful in their words and deeds, particularly when speaking to other people.

The next essential value and attitude to apply in interpersonal communication is justice.

> *"Be just, that is nearer to righteousness" (Quran 5:8)*

This verse highlights the great importance of fairness in interpersonal relationships by not only urging people to act justly but also emphasising that justice and righteousness go hand in hand.

Numerous other qualities serve as the cornerstone for courteous and meaningful interpersonal contact. Islam encourages relationships to be founded on kindness and respect for one another, even in the face of cruel treatment. True believers show their dedication to speaking kindly and remaining composed in the face of injustice and hostility by responding to harshness with words of peace.

From the spread of religious teachings (dakwah) to different types of public communication, Islamic ethics are essential in directing communication across a wide variety of activities and goals. Most common core communication ethics principles are included in the Islamic perspective, including:

- The Tauhid concept, which highlights the core purpose and essence of communication development;
- The idea of controlling uplifting information without influencing opinions
- The idea of being truthful and refraining from lying in order to build trust; and

These Islamic communication ideas and guidelines emphasise the value of moral communication within the framework of Islam and its wider social ramifications.

Chapter Five

Building and Nurturing Friendships

Building Strong Foundations in Friendship

One of the most significant relationships we will ever form is with our friends, and a good friendship cannot develop without the right support and care. More than merely social ties, friendships are essential to our wellbeing because they provide us with joy, support, and a feeling of community. But not every friendship improves our quality of life.

We can develop the kind of friendships that enhance our lives and promote personal development if we're aware of the differences between good and unhealthy relationships. For healthy friendships to truly take root and thrive, a combination of a few qualities is required for building a strong foundation. Let's examine the fundamentals of establishing strong friendships and preserving them throughout time.

Establishing Trust in Friendship

A good friendship or relationship is built on trust, which calls for both parties to be prepared to put efforts into the partnership. It's a quality that is difficult to acquire yet simple to lose. Being trustworthy in a relationship entails being truthful, dependable, and communicative with your companion.

Building solid associations requires trust, a basic component of all interactions. It's the conviction that the other individual will be trustworthy, honest, and considerate of your interests. When you trust someone, you know you can rely on them in times of need and feel secure and confident with them. It's critical to remember that trust cannot be taken for granted. It needs to be earned gradually via open and sincere communication.

It also calls for mutual understanding and support during difficult times, as well as the ability to forgive and accept faults. A relationship built on trust thrives and offers a secure environment where both parties may freely and honestly express themselves without fear of criticism. By being forthright and honest with one another, friends might gain a greater knowledge and respect for one another.

Amana, which comes from the Arabic root "A-M-N," which meaning to be safe or secure, represents a dedication to carrying out duties honestly and responsibly. "Amana" means trust, and it's significant in Islam because it embodies the concepts of integrity and accountability.

This idea has significant ramifications for both individual behaviour and interpersonal interactions, and it's firmly anchored in Islamic beliefs. Amana is the term used to describe any kind of trust or obligation given to a person. It includes many facets of life, including friendship.

The significance of Amana is emphasised in multiple verses of the Quran. For example, Allah (SWT) commands believers to return trust to their rightful owners and to be just in their dealings (Quran 4:58).

In his teachings, the Prophet Muhammad (PBUH) further emphasised the importance of Amana, saying that a sincere believer maintains the obligations and trusts.

> *He said, "When a man tells something and he intends it to be a trust, then it is a trust". (Sunah Abu Dawud)*

In Islam, friendship must also be based on "Ikhlas" (sincere care for the welfare of others). True friends should always look out for each other's best interests and never have hidden agendas. Muslims are encouraged to be dependable and trustworthy in their social relationships to keep their friends' trust and confide in them about important matters.

Hazrat Abu Bakr (RA) was adored and revered by the Prophet (PBUH), who regarded him as a devoted companion who stood by him no matter what that's why the Prophet (PBUH) called Abu Bakr (RA) "My Companion" and "My Friend" due to that close bond. Sincere friendships are founded on devotion to Allah (SWT), trust, and loyalty, and their bond serves as the best example for us.

Role of Open Communication in Friendship

Open communication is essential to any successful and healthy relationship. It allows people to exchange information, thoughts, and sentiments in both directions and is an essential part of developing mutual understanding. When both people are at ease expressing their ideas and feelings without worrying about criticism or negative consequences, they create a safe and encouraging environment for progress and growth.

People can freely communicate their needs, wants, and worries as a result, which improves mutual understanding of needs and viewpoints. The development of honesty and openness between people is one of the most important advantages of open communication. The quality and depth of our friendships are influenced by the way we communicate with one another. The most crucial thing to know about healthy relationships in general is that they are constructed rather than magically created.

For the people we are in connection with to understand us and, in turn, support us in the ways we require, we must be willing to be vulnerable enough to speak and express ourselves to establish a good relationship. You invite someone into your life and inner world when you speak. You are giving them important details that will enable them to comprehend your emotional requirements.

Openness, like a book with all the pages spread wide for your friend to read, is the foundation of open communication. It is a superpower in friendships, the glue that keeps them together. It's crucial because it fosters deep emotional ties and trust between friends.

Consider keeping a secret that you're afraid to share with anyone. Eventually, telling your friends about it seems like a burden is lifted, and they sympathise and encourage you. This strengthens and deepens your bond, which is the power of open conversation.

In Islam, the value of excellent communication is highly emphasised. The eternal teachings on communication tactics found in the Quran and sayings of Prophet Muhammad (PBUH), and Seerah (the life of the Prophet (PBUH)) are still very applicable today. These resources include ethical, courteous, and powerful communication guidelines that help improve our relationships and successfully and clearly communicate ideas.

What kind of communication did the Prophet (PBUH) have with his companions? What does this teach us? Allah (SWT) gave the Prophet (PBUH) and his Ummah instructions in the Quran itself to communicate by selecting the most appropriate phrases, saying:

"Tell my servants to say what is best." (Quran 17:53)

This isn't an easy task because humans are talkative creatures and do not always consider what we say. Additionally, this does not imply that, as is often the case in many conversations, we polish our blades as if we were going to combat every time we speak. Instead, try your best to use words that will express a positive meaning in the most considerate manner when you speak. Nonetheless, we must emulate the Prophet (PBUH) since he is the ideal example, and we must try to align our own character with his as much as possible. Let's talk about some of the essential manners that Hazrat Muhammad (PBUH) demonstrated when communicating with others during His life:

Act of smiling

Except in situations where He (PBUH) witnessed wrongdoing, the Allah Almighty's Holy Prophet (PBUH) always had a positive expression to the people he met. Because Prophet Muhammad (PBUH) always acted in a welcoming manner, it demonstrates that maintaining a smile is an open invitation to others for conversation and a sign of goodwill. Being receptive to everyone is a terrific way to share your message at anytime and anywhere.

A grin is a great way to dispel any residual negative thoughts and start a conversation in a pleasant manner. Make it a habit to start a conversation with a smile, ask Allah (SWT) for wisdom and goodness, and enter with a peaceful heart. Even when one person is depressed, anxious, or angry, you'll be shocked at how much positive energy it can bring to the table.

> *Abdullah ibn Al-Harith ibn Hazm said, "I have never seen anyone who smiles more than the Prophet does." (Tirmidhi) In addition, Prophet (PBUH) said, "Smiling in your brother's face is an act of charity" (Tirmidhi)*

Wishing Peace to Others

It is advised to say "Salam" and shake hands with friends before starting communication. Saying "Assalaamu alaykum wa rahmatullahi wa barakatuh" (peace be upon you and may Allah's kindness and blessings be upon you) is a must for everyone to express empathy. In the same vein, concluding the talk with "Salam" promotes a constructive conclusion to any dialogue.

In Islam, shaking hands with someone of the same gender is advised. By doing this, you can gain the trust of others and it's also highly valued as a way for Muslims to have positive relationships with one another and win Allah's (SWT) mercy.

Truthfulness and Honesty

The Prophet Muhammad (PBUH) emphasised the need to be truthful when speaking to anyone. Because of his dedication to honesty, he was called as "Al-Amin" (The Trustworthy). He emphasised that while dishonesty produces devastation, honesty provides blessings, and his words were never misleading.

> *"Truthfulness leads to righteousness, and righteousness leads to Paradise. A man keeps on telling the truth until he becomes a truthful person, Falsehood leads to wickedness, and wickedness leads to Hellfire."* (Bukhari)

Speaking the truth at all times, especially when it's challenging, is basic principle of communication emphasised in the Quran.

> *"O you who have believed, fear Allah and speak words of appropriate justice." (Quran 33:70)*

Manage your Tone and Volume

When conversing with someone, remember that you're in charge of the words you use and the emotions you bring up in them. In addition to producing positive outcomes, having polite, respectful talks will also earn you rewards from Allah (SWT). When speaking, pay attention to the tone and volume of your voice. To make your point, don't raise your voice. Choose phrases that will more politely and respectfully convey your thoughts and feelings instead. When conversing with friends or others, show consideration for their rank and position.

> *"And be moderate in your pace and lower your voice; indeed, the most disagreeable of sounds is the voice of donkeys." (Quran: 31:19)*

To ensure that the conversation is pertinent and the other person understands, it's important to utilise clear language and expressions when conversing with them. Speaking eloquently was always the Holy Prophet's (PBUH) best practice while communicating.

Additionally, be clear in your voice. People may not understand you if you speak incoherently, and you may become irritated if they disregard your words. It needlessly causes friction. Thus, make your communication easy to grasp, clear and succinct.

Hazrat Aisha (RA) explained the Holy Prophet's (PBUH) speech patterns. He didn't babble on and on as some people do, she said. Some folks talk so fast they don't even stop to catch their breath. They do not give you a chance to speak, and it's difficult to follow what they are saying. In contrast, the Sunnah is not like this; the Prophet (PBUH) spoke plainly and slowly. If you talk too quickly, take a moment to breathe, pause, and speak more slowly—not too slowly, just at a speed that makes sense to listeners.

> *Aisha (RA) said "The Messenger of Allah (PBUH) did not speak quickly like you do now, rather he would speak so clearly, unmistakably, that those who sat with him would memorise it." (Tirmidhi)*

Use Positive and Encouraging Words

When speaking to others, the Prophet Muhammad (PBUH) always employed words that were uplifting, encouraging, and positive. He understood how effective praise and positive reinforcement could be in inspiring others.

Instead of giving harsh criticism, the Prophet (PBUH) would gently point them toward improved behaviour. His use of affectionate language, such as referring to his friends by titles or nicknames that conveyed love and respect, is an illustration of this.

> *"He who does not show mercy to our young ones and does not realise the right of our elders is not from us"*
> *(Sunah Abi Dawud)*

Avoiding Unnecessary Arguing

As mentioned above, a true Muslim's life is characterised by the positive use of language, yet occasionally, during conversation, things spiral out of control and result in harsh remarks, which is prohibited in Islam. It's best to stay upbeat during conversations and, if your friend is upset, try to listen carefully and treat the issue with extreme caution. This is because meaningless arguments lead to conflicts and arguments, which cause one to lose consciousness and get irritated.

Hazrat Muhammad (PBUH) demonstrated profound knowledge and always maintained composure in the face of conflict.

> *Once a man said to the Prophet (PBUH), "Advise me," and he said, "Do not get angry." He repeated his question several times and again the Prophet (PBUH) said: "Do not get angry." (Sahih Bukhari)*

Listen Actively and Respect the Opinion of Others

Effective communication involves carefully listening to others and allowing them to express themselves. The Prophet Muhammad's (PBUH) conversational style is evident in his Seerah. He never interrupted others when they were speaking and always listened intently. Respect and understanding are fostered when others receive your undivided attention.

> *"When the Prophet would turn to speak to someone, he would turn his whole body towards them and give them his full attention" (Sunah Abu Dawud)*

This demonstrates that respecting the speaker and actively listening are crucial elements of communication.

Thus, strong friendships can be built on open communication because it promotes trust, understanding, and emotional ties. By freely sharing their ideas and emotions, friends foster a safe environment for support and development. Effective communication, as exemplified by Prophet Muhammad (PBUH), should be courteous, truthful, and kind to improve relationships and fortify ties.

Nurturing Healthy Friendships Over Time

One of life's greatest treasures might be a friendship. Maintaining and fostering these relationships might become increasingly difficult as we age because of shifting goals, growing responsibilities, and changing life circumstances. Some people want more friendships, while others are content with a small network of friends.

Maintaining close, genuine friendships has incalculable benefits. It's crucial to consider the value of solid connections in preserving and enhancing our mental well-being. Close connections can improve our lives in a variety of ways, from assisting with relaxation to acting as an emotional support system. Lifelong friendships require care and attention, just like any other relationship. Here are a few strategies for fostering friendships that last a lifetime.

Strategies for Maintaining Bonds of Friendship

Here are some guidelines that address every spiritual, emotional, and practical element that each of us should strive to inculcate in our lives and relationships:

Start with Imaan, Taqwa and Selfless Love

Any tie must have a solid foundation to flourish; anything must have a strong base to endure over time, and for you, and for Muslims that foundation is our Creator Allah (SWT). Ensure that the focus of your friendship is Allah (SWT). Unless it's for His sake alone, you won't be able to appreciate the deliciousness of this bundle of delight and its true beauty. Relationships that are conscious of the Almighty are essential because the people we spend our time with significantly impact us.

We Muslims know that the secret to success in this life and the next is realising the Tawheed (Oneness of the Creator of the universe), which entails remembering God the Exalted constantly and carrying out all His directives. We should endeavour to establish and maintain relationships that help us carry out our first duty of remembering the Almighty since we're also conscious of the strain our peers may put on us. Strengthen your bond by seeking love from the correct source, Al Wadood (The Ever Loving), and nourish it with the light of Imaan and the pearls of Taqwa is necessary.

> *The Prophet (PBUH) said: "A man follows the religion of his friend; so each one should consider whom he makes his friend." (Abu Dawud)*

Accept Changing Dynamics

Accepting the reality of changing dynamics is the next step in preserving friendships when priorities change. Recognise that your priorities and your friends' may shift as life progresses. Approach these changes with openness and acceptance rather than resistance. Acknowledge that friendships inevitably evolve, and be prepared to adjust to new situations when they come up.

Be there and be around. In a world of technology, hectic schedules, home, office, college, and family, friends can occasionally go neglected. Avoid falling into this category. Be someone who is accessible in an emergency. When your friend is unable to stand, hold their hand, offer them support during difficult times, and attempt to restore the smiles that have been lost.

Furthermore, you must be accountable for what you have been trusted with and not disregard dependability. Don't allow irresponsibility to separate you from your best friend. Take everything seriously; if something needs to be done, be there on time, and don't let your friend think you're just brilliant at meaningless conversations and that you're a loser when it comes to action plans. Lead by example!

Accept Common Interests

Friendships are firmly based on shared interests and experiences. Spend time doing activities you both enjoy, whether it's hiking, joining a book club, taking cooking classes, visiting mosques, or taking trips together. As well as creating new experiences together, trying out new hobbies can change the dynamic of your friendship.

Be a Motivating "Sadeeq"

Be that extraordinary person who encourages their friends to pursue their dreams and achieve their objectives. No one knows your friends' strengths and abilities better than you, so serve as their mentor and advisor. Persuade them and entice them with the magnificent rewards intended for the true believers who stand out and accomplish something beyond comprehension for the Ummah.

Be Understanding and Adaptable

Maintaining friendships when priorities change requires flexibility. Recognise that your friends might occasionally have obligations and duties that take precedence. Be accommodating of alterations to plans or routines and flexible in your expectations.

Develop compassion and understanding for your friends' situations, offering support and encouragement whenever you can. Share your thoughts, ideas, and worries, and urge them to do the same. By fostering honest communication, you can align expectations and strengthen your connection.

Think and Be Grateful

Give your friendships some thought and acknowledge their importance in your life. Thank your friends for being there for you and supporting you. Every now and again, travel back in time and remember the moments you've spent together. It strengthens the relationship and instills feelings of appreciation and nostalgia.

Honour Differences and Boundaries

Each person has their own limitations and distinctions. To keep your friendship balanced and healthy, abide by these. Recognise that having diverse beliefs, passions, or ways of living is acceptable. Develop empathy and active listening skills to comprehend your friend's viewpoint without passing judgement.

Be Understanding and Encouraging

The journey of life is full of ups and downs. Celebrate your friends' victories and support them through their difficult moments. Your relationship is strengthened when you're a trustworthy source of understanding and support. Small acts of kindness, such as offering assistance or sending a kind message, can make a big difference in demonstrating your support.

Thus, as you age maintaining friendships takes work, perseverance, and a sincere desire to stay in touch. Recall that friendships enrich our lives by bringing solace, happiness, and a feeling of community. They'll be a source of strength and joy for the rest of your life if you invest and treasure them.

Chapter Six

Loyalty and Support in Friendship

Importance of Loyalty (Wafa) in Friendships

For Muslims, loyalty to Allah (SWT) always comes first. However, this is only possible if they follow His instructions.

Allah says: "Do not be like those who forgot Allah so He made them forget themselves. Such people are the deviators" (Quran 59:19)

Loyalty to the Messenger of Allah (PBUH) is the highest and most essential kind of loyalty after devotion to Allah (SWT). This devotion is a way to show appreciation for the Prophet Muhammad (PBUH), who always prioritised his community in his prayers to Allah (SWT). Devotion to the Prophet's (PBUH) Sunnah enables this loyalty, which starts as one's affection for him grows.

Loyalty is regarded as one of Islam's most important moral traits, and it plays a crucial role in all aspects of our lives and relationships. Loyalty to the great men of our religion, or Islam companions, should also be a part of every Muslim believer's heart. So, loyalty is regarded as one of Islam's most important moral traits. We need to cultivate a sense of loyalty towards our religious brothers and sisters and companions. Furthermore, good character and personality traits include loyalty to our ancestors, our nation, our surviving and deceased, and the trusts placed in our care.

Loyalty (Wafa) in friendships involves steadfast support and allegiance to each other, even in challenging times. It means standing by your friend's side, respecting their needs, and maintaining trust despite obstacles. A friend's loyalty is an excellent virtue. When loyalty in a friendship is missing, other values will indeed suffer in any relationship.

As we have limited time on our hands between all of life's responsibilities. Sometimes friendship gets pushed to the bottom of the priority list. We may find ourselves choosing friends who aren't loyal out of convenience. But remember, loyalty between friends will hold the bond for the long haul.

Knowing we have someone we can always rely on is what gives us a sense of security—the unspoken commitment. Loyal friendships endure through life's ups and downs, providing an incomparable sense of trust and belonging. When there is loyalty, a connection is formed that endures beyond space and time, strengthening and deepening the link.

Emotional intimacy is another benefit of loyalty. You are more inclined to be open and honest with someone when you have faith that they would support you. This strengthens the friendship over time and creates an unbreakable tie. Conversely, lacking devotion breeds mistrust and emotional detachment, which can swiftly terminate friendships.

According to one of Imam Ali's (AS) Arabic hadiths, loyalty is the most respectable quality. Imam Ali (AS) emphasises the importance and dignity of loyalty in this lovely Hadith.

> *"Righteousness is not that you turn your faces toward the east or the west, but [true] righteousness is [in] one who believes in Allah, the Last Day, the angels, the Book, and the prophets and gives wealth, in spite of love for it, to relatives, orphans, the needy, the traveler, those who ask [for help], and for freeing slaves; [and who] establishes prayer and gives zakah; [those who] fulfill their promise when they promise; and [those who] are patient in poverty and hardship and during battle. Those are the ones who have been true, and it is those who are the righteous." (Quran 2:177)*

This verse emphasises that genuine righteousness involves keeping one's word, being faithful to one's obligations, and acting morally. Those who are truly just in Allah's (SWT) eyes exhibit loyalty, a necessary component of righteousness.

Prophetic Examples of Loyalty and Steadfastness

Among the other beautiful traits of the Holy Prophet (PBUH), very known for winning hearts of others, were his loyalty, truthfulness, keeping promises, and restoring trusts to their rightful owners.

The Quran affirms the significance of these qualities, as Almighty Allah (SWT) states:

> *"And do not come near the wealth of the orphan—unless intending to enhance it—until they attain maturity. Give full measure and weigh with justice. We never require of any soul more than what it can afford. Whenever you speak, maintain justice—even regarding a close relative. And fulfill your covenant with Allah. This is what He has commanded you, so perhaps you will be mindful." (Quran 6:152)*

The noble trait Loyalty can be seen in the way the Prophet (PBUH) worshipped Allah (SWT) and interacted with his wife, friends, and even adversaries. He was faithful and honest in his delivery of the message that the Lord had given him. He explained Islam to the populace and led them along the straight and narrow path in accordance with Allah's (SWT) instructions.

Moreover, the Holy Prophet (PBUH) stayed faithful to his wife Khadija (RA) and was grateful for her sacrifices, generosity, wisdom, and strong position. Even after her passing, he continued to speak of her and recalled her deeds. He was faithful to her and used to visit her family and show kindness to her friends.

The Holy Prophet (PBUH) was faithful to all his other wives and family. He never forgot the care his uncle provided after he was orphaned at eight and continued to support him throughout his life. Even after his uncle's passing, he continued to pray for Allah's (SWT) forgiveness.

The Holy Prophet (PBUH) was also devoted to all living things. He used to walk every day from his mosque chamber to the pulpit, where he led Muslims in prayer. There were a few stairs between his mosque room and the pulpit. He cherished those meters of ground since they led to Allah (SWT) and his favourite activity, prayer.

Thus, the loyalty that the Holy Prophet (PBUH) displayed toward others during his life reflects the deep sense of gratitude and faithfulness that defined his character. Likewise, despite immense challenges, his steadfastness in upholding the message of Islam remains an enduring inspiration.

The examples of his loyalty serve as a guiding light, reminding us that true faith is not only about belief but also about fulfilling our responsibilities with sincerity, honesty, and devotion. His unwavering commitment to truth, trust, and justice set a standard for all believers.

Benefits of Standing by Friends in Times of Adversity and Joy

True friendship is revealed throughout difficult periods in life. Loyalty is demonstrated when a true friend sticks by you through difficult times. In Islam, standing by friends when they need you the most, in times of adversity and joy, is highly encouraged and carries great rewards. Some connections wane when times get difficult but true friendships always endure. This is the real moment when friendships create togetherness and build ties. Here are a few main advantages:

Gaining Allah's (SWT) Pleasure and Rewards

There are many occasions when others ask for assistance, perhaps in the form of counsel, advice, or simply a simple favour. We frequently feel hesitant, worn out, or contemptuous, believing the issue is too unimportant to merit our time. But as Surah Al-Mujadila so eloquently reminds us, even the little deeds of compassion can result in great blessings. Allah (SWT) teaches us the great value of giving and helping others in this verse.

By doing so, we not only ease their lives but also open the door to numerous blessings and comfort in our own lives, both here on Earth and in the hereafter. The underlying lesson, however, is clear: even a small act of kindness can lead to greater blessings from Allah (SWT). Allah (SWT) promises to enhance our standing in both knowledge and faith if we humble ourselves and act charitably.

> *"O you who have believed, when you are told to make space in gatherings, then make space; Allah will make space for you. And when you are told to rise, then rise; Allah will raise those who have believed among you and those who were given knowledge, by degrees. And Allah is acquainted with what you do." (Quran 58:11)*

It is believed that one technique to establish, preserve, and fortify your social ties is to assist your friends in their hard times. As Muslims we believe that one might gain Allah's (SWT) mercy and blessings by helping and caring for friends, particularly during trying times.

> *"The most beloved people to Allah are those who are most beneficial to others." (Al-Mujam Al-Awsat)*

Earning Support in Times of Need

Helping friends ensures that they'll also stand by us when we face difficulties. Sustaining solid and encouraging friendships requires knowing how to support your friends during difficult times. Problems are common, and friends serve as our network of support. Big or small, our assistance counts when they are going through difficult times.

Life is full of unexpected turns and twists. When times are difficult, we frequently turn to our friends first. Offering assistance can make a difference, whether friends are struggling, going through a personal crisis, experiencing a significant life transition, or just feeling overburdened.

> *"Whoever relieves a believer's distress, Allah will relieve his distress on the Day of Judgment." (Sahih Muslim)*

Moreover, supporting friends during hardships and celebrating their joys reflects true Islamic character, demonstrating sincerity and good morals.

> *"None of you truly believes until he loves for his brother what he loves for himself." (Sahih Bukhari)*

Islam also promotes emotional and mental well-being by encouraging believers to support one another, reducing stress and loneliness. Even a simple smile is considered an act of charity. Ultimately, standing by friends in both hardship and joy is not only a moral duty but a path to spiritual success in this life and the hereafter.

Providing Emotional and Spiritual Support

Social and emotional support is vital to human life and well-being. Islamic psychology also emphasises its importance, aligning with the teachings of the Quran and the life of the Holy Prophet (PBUH). In Islamic psychology, providing any type of assistance to enhance someone's spiritual life is referred to as social support.

It's critical to comprehend your own spiritual beliefs to provide spiritual support to others. Consider a period of your life when you had to deal with a significant loss, change, or transition.

During that period, did you find spiritual strength?

What spiritual effects did it have on you?

What impact did your faith have on the encounter?

In what way did you wish to receive spiritual support?

Have you ever doubted your religious beliefs?

Exploring these issues will enhance your understanding of your spirituality amidst life-altering circumstances, even if you have not been personally diagnosed with a serious disorder. Spiritual experiences and beliefs can differ significantly, even within communities, families, and circles of friends. Clearly indicate that your principles and viewpoints solely reflect your own. Your friend or family member desires you to listen to them with the same reverence and understanding that you would wish to receive from someone else.

Role of Empathy and Encouragement in Supporting Friends' Well-being

The capacity to experience another person's feelings and perceive things from their perspective is known as empathy. By putting yourself in another person's shoes, you can respond empathetically and strive to improve their circumstances. In doing so, you can alleviate both your own distress and that of the other person.

If your friend is upset with the treatment they received from others, you'll most likely share their feelings. You may realise that they need to vent their feelings, even if you're unable to address their problem. Empathy allows you to deepen your relationships with friends and loved ones because you can relate to their thoughts and feelings, and they can relate to yours.

Sympathy and empathy are two distinct concepts. Unlike empathy, sympathy does not require deep consideration for another person's feelings. You are empathetic when you care about someone's problem or misfortune and feel sorrow for their pain, even if you don't fully grasp their anguish.

For instance, one might empathise with a friend who has lost someone dear to them and understand their grief. However, it's also possible to share in their sadness through empathy. Sympathy is often viewed as a more melancholic emotion, whereas empathy embodies a sense of compassion for the individual.

Islam encourages empathy as a fundamental virtue. Compassion and empathy are regarded as significant Islamic virtues and are promoted in various ways across the faith. Being empathetic will make you a more helpful person, enhance your relationships, and help you grow as a Muslim. The Prophet (PBUH) himself reportedly urged us to develop empathy for one another by saying:

> "The believers in their mutual kindness, compassion and sympathy are just like one body. When one of the limbs suffers, the whole body responds to it with wakefulness and fever." (Sahih Bukhari)

Prophet Muhammad (PBUH) was kind, understanding, and loving. He cared for the material and spiritual well-being of his friends, family, and everyone else around him, doing everything in his power to ensure their welfare. He nurtured them and consistently considered their fate in the afterlife, encouraging them to uphold their moral principles.

> "A Messenger has come to you from among yourselves. Your suffering is distressing to him; he is deeply concerned for you; he is gentle and merciful to the believers." (Quran 9:128)

> "And lower your wing (in kindness) unto those believers who follow you" (Quran 26:215)

Muslims are constantly instructed by the Quran to be empathetic and sympathetic. Here is how Quran highlight the value of compassion and empathy:

> "And what will make you realise what 'attempting' the challenging path is? It is to pay debts on behalf of others or to give food in times of famine, to an orphaned relative, or to a poor person in distress, and—above all—to be one of those who have faith and urge each other to perseverance and urge each other to compassion. (Quran 90:12-17)

So, empathy acts as a beacon of light in times of need, showing the way to assistance and motivation. Empathy enables you to provide sympathetic assistance, such as a listening ear, a shoulder to rely on, or words of encouragement, when a friend is going through difficulties or disappointments. You give your friend the courage and confidence they need to face challenging situations by acknowledging their emotions and providing empathy-driven support. The idea that no one is struggling alone is reinforced, and this constant support strengthens the friendship between friends.

Chapter Seven

Challenges in Friendships and Their Resolutions

Common Challenges in Friendships

Having a strong connection can be incredibly fulfilling, but it's natural for challenges to come up along the way. Even the strongest friendships can face difficulties.

Remember, it's perfectly normal to disagree now and then. While experiencing a rift with someone close to your heart can be tough, it doesn't mean your friendship has to end.

After a disagreement, it's normal for things to feel slightly off for a while. You might find yourself wondering if you even want to mend your friendship or how to go about it.

It's common to encounter some bumps in the road in a healthy connection. By being aware of these potential issues, you can take steps to address them quickly and keep your friendship.

Dealing with Conflicts and Misunderstandings

Human connection inevitably entails conflict; thus, acquiring healthy and productive conflict resolution techniques is critical, particularly when a close friend is involved. Essentially, to collide with someone or something is termed conflict. Disagreement over differing viewpoints serves as an example of conflict. Avoiding disagreement is not the aim of friendship. True friendship strives to manage disagreement and prevent dysfunction.

The Sunnah and the Quran exhort Muslim believers to promote peace. The fundamental essence of Islam is peace. A sincere believer is filled with inner serenity and contentment. This tranquilly then radiates outward, bringing hope and contentment to society.

The development of individual character and the communal virtues of justice and fraternity are among the ultimate goals of Shariah. Muslims have been ordained by Allah (SWT) to be brothers, and upholding that bond guarantees His kindness. On the other hand, Muslims must mediate disputes or conflicts and strive to settle them amicably and as quickly as possible.

Numerous examples of re-establishing justice and harmony are found in various aspects of life in the Quran and the Sunnah, and these approaches to reconciliation remain relevant today. The Sunnah provides instances of how these teachings have been applied, while the Quran sets forth guidelines for addressing disagreements.

Allah (SWT) commands the believers to settle their disagreements and conflicts with one another in a friendly manner, prohibits them from engaging in combat with one another, and forewarns them that failing to do so will cause them to lose their power as a society.

"And reconcile your mutual differences." (Quran 8:1)

> "And dispute not with one another, then you will lose courage by getting demoralised and your strength will be lost." (Quran 8:46)

Similarly Prophet Muhammad (PBUH) faced numerous difficulties during his lifetime, which he handled in the most exquisite way. Every dispute he settled serves as a model for all of humanity.

There is an urgent need to highlight relevant examples from the seerah of Prophet Muhammad (PBUH) where he effectively resolved disputes between conflicting parties to encourage reconciliation.

Disagreements among Prophet Muhammad's (PBUH) wives or associates occasionally escalated into confrontations. The disputing parties protested to the Holy Prophet (PBUH) about the other, and he determined which of them was at fault. He needed to make amends or pay the other by using objective judgement and wisdom inspired by Allah (SWT).

Hazrat Abu Bakr (RA) and Hazrat Umar (RA) were dear friends who had once gotten into a fight. Hazrat Umar (RA) felt upset about something that had happened involving Hazrat Abu Bakr (RA). When Hazrat Abu Bakr (RA) joined the Holy Prophet (PBUH) and his companions, including the narrator Abud Darda, the Prophet (PBUH) noticed right away that Hazrat Abu Bakr (RA) seemed a bit uneasy, likely because of his facial expression and body language. However, the Prophet (PBUH) chose to remain silent. It wasn't until Hazrat Umar (RA) came in and shared his side of the story with the Prophet (PBUH) that things took a turn.

The Prophet (PBUH) grew enraged upon learning the specifics of this debate. When Hazrat Abu Bakr (RA) saw the Prophet's (PBUH) discomfort, he instantly acknowledged that he was more to blame. The Prophet (PBUH) devised a two-step plan to persuade Hazrat Umar

(RA) to pardon him after observing that Hazrat Abu Bakr (RA) had not only acknowledged his own mistakes but also asked for forgiveness.

He began by referring to Hazrat Abu Bakr (RA) as his companion and twice asked everyone seated around him whether they would "leave" for him his friend, meaning they would part from the one person who had always supported him. This statement illustrates how Hazrat Abu Bakr (RA) demonstrated his devotion to Allah (SWT) as the Prophet's (PBUH) friend and supporter, particularly in times of hardship.

To illustrate Hazrat Abu Bakr's (RA) sincerity and devotion to the truth to those gathered around him, the Prophet (PBUH) recounted how, when he first began to proclaim his prophetic status to humanity, he was called a liar by everyone except Hazrat Abu Bakr (RA), who responded, "You speak the truth."

When resolving conflicts, this story teaches us the value of being quick to forgive someone who sincerely acknowledges their mistakes and earnestly asks for our forgiveness. It can be helpful to remind the victim of the positive things the wrongdoer has done in the past, especially when there's clear evidence that the offender is truly honest, sincere, and moral. Letting anger linger shouldn't keep us apart from those who have shown their genuine commitment to us.

However, there are a number of reasons why disagreements and miscommunications may occur. To effectively address these issues, it's imperative to comprehend their underlying causes. A communication breakdown is one of the primary causes of disagreements and miscommunications in friendships. Friends frequently struggle to articulate their views or feelings precisely, which can result in miscommunications. Open and honest communication with your friend is essential.

Disparities in expectations are another frequent reason why friendships fail. Everyone has different expectations for friendships, and when those standards are not met, it can lead to dissatisfaction and conflict. Engaging in conversation with your friend to clarify expectations is essential. This involves respecting each other's needs and establishing boundaries, such as personal time and space. Clearly defining expectations may help prevent misunderstandings and enhance your relationship connection.

Conflict frequently arises from misconceptions or a lack of knowledge. It occurs frequently in cross-cultural conflicts when communication is inadequate and presumptions are incorrect. However, information issues can arise at any time. People may become angry with one another due to inadequate or missing context or a variety of other information-related issues.

Cutting off communication is a typical reaction when people are at odds with someone else. Although it may seem like a decent method to keep a problem from getting worse, refusing to talk is only a temporary solution. In the long run, it usually makes matters worse. Without communication, misconceptions remain unresolved, the issue festers, and interpersonal relationships and teamwork are disrupted.

Recognising Causes and Applying Strategies for Resolving Conflicts

Spend some time conversing with your friend and learning about his or her perspective if it's only a small miscommunication. But if it's a big argument, you might need to consider how important this connection is to you and if you're willing to try to keep it going. Determine the problematic scenario that you wish to alter right now, and then communicate your feelings. With your friend, determine what must be altered to maintain a polite and healthy connection.

Setting and timing are important when discussing delicate topics. Choose a quiet, cosy area where you two can talk freely about the issue without interruptions. Choose a moment when you're both somewhat at ease and open to talking.

Turn the topic of discussion to the advantages of your friendship. Remind one another of the enjoyable moments and common experiences that have strengthened your bond. Reiterate the importance of the friendship and say that you want to put the miscommunication behind you.

No individual is ever entirely to blame for a quarrel. The other person will be more inclined to listen if you acknowledge your mistakes. Engage in the dispute resolution process. Show your willingness to collaborate with your friend to find solutions, make amends, and express your openness and interest in understanding their perspective. Assess the options collectively. Are they practical? Do both of you find them satisfactory? Which is the most effective in resolving the issue? Next, reach a consensus and commit to upholding it.

Offer your heartfelt apologies if you believe what you did caused the misunderstanding. Accepting responsibility for your actions demonstrates maturity and a desire to repair the friendship. Additionally, if your friend apologises, be ready to forgive them. Rebuilding trust and moving on require forgiveness. Giving each other time and space to think things through is sometimes essential. Give your friend time to absorb the discussion and the conclusion. Tension can increase if the healing process is rushed.

It takes time and persistent work to rebuild trust. Show each other that you're dedicated to keeping the friendship going by being patient with one another. Rebuilding trust can be greatly aided by small acts of compassion and understanding. You can repair your friendship and cultivate an even closer bond by being honest about the issue, apologising, forgiving, and setting boundaries.

Peacemaking Principles According to Islam

Islam literally translates to two fundamental ideas: First of all, Islam is derived from the Arabic term "Salima/Yaslemu" which means to "submit or surrender to Allah (SWT)". Furthermore, the Arabic noun "Salam" signifies peace or the acquisition of peace. Islam provides a thorough framework for preserving wholesome relationships by emphasising fundamental principles like justice, forgiveness, compassion, and respect.

These tenets offer insightful guidance for settling disputes and fostering closer friendships. A few interconnected Islamic concepts that Prophet Muhammad (PBUH) used in advancing his idea of good peace during his lifetime are at the heart of this Islamic ecosystem of peacemaking. Let's have a look on these in detail:

The Seven Principles are:

Tawhid, the faith in Allah (SWT), is the main tenet guiding Islam's approach to peace.

"Humanity is a single community" (Quran 2:213)

which arises from a single source in which all individuals are infused with the same elements, is a corollary of God's unity. This idea of humanity's togetherness is a potent defence against conflict and separation. The assurance to guarantee the inclusion of all creation in peacemaking and transformational statecraft processes comes from this transcendent unity and its human manifestation.

Since establishing earthly and heavenly oneness is a major goal of God's cosmos, unity serves as both the goal and the reason for humanity's existence on Earth. Because unity is essential, Islam cannot be apathetic or disinterested when it comes to promoting peace; aiming only for adverse peace or the avoidance of conflict is insufficient. If this idea is to be fulfilled, Islam demands a far more positive condition of being expressed in the manner of harmonious integration of all societal aspects.

Islam places a high value on pursuing peace, or "Silm", which is the foundation of the Islamic peace building ecosystem. Since its success, development, humanism, and integrity depend on its good presence, the Muslim community cannot exist without it.

> *"Oh believers: enter into Silm wholeheartedly!" (Quran 2:208)*

The Prophet (PBUH) tells Muslims to avoid violence and to establish peace in numerous sayings.

> *"Shall I inform you of a better act than fasting, alms, and prayers? Make peace between one another: enmity and malice tear up heavenly rewards by roots." (Tirmidhi)*

> *"If the enemy is inclined towards peace, make peace with them. And put your trust in Allah. Indeed, He alone is the All-Hearing, All-Knowing." (Quran 8:61)*

The integrity and unity of all creation rely on the justice "Adl" principle, another fundamental value. Many of the Quran's lessons focus on empowering people to coexist peacefully and execute their duties to one another to maintain justice and everyone's well-being. Justice fully handling complaints guarantees that disputes are settled fairly, promoting enduring peace.

Islamic principles are based on respect. The Quran commands us to converse with honour and dignity regardless of differences. Respecting one another's opinions, emotions, and boundaries during disagreements encourages healthy communication and mutual understanding. A core tenet of Islam is that forgiveness is necessary for settling conflicts. In his dealings with others, the Prophet Muhammad (PBUH) was a living example of forgiveness; he frequently pardoned individuals who had offended him. Practicing forgiveness entails letting go of grudges and pursuing the resolution with compassion, not ignoring the current problems.

Seeking Mediation (Shura) for Maintaining Harmony

Islam promotes mediation as a means of resolving conflicts. Mediation involves an impartial third party, which can help when friends cannot resolve conflicts on their own. A recognised person, such as an elder or community leader, who can lead the discussion and assist in identifying points of agreement, should serve as the mediator.

Mediation is a ray of hope that provides a means of resolving conflicts and fostering reconciliation. Islamic mediation, rooted in justice, empathy, and compassion, offers a traditional method of resolving disputes that promotes peace and understanding between people and communities.

> *The Quran exhorts Muslims to pursue peace and reconciliation as: "repel evil with good" (Quran 7:199) and to "make peace between your brothers." (Quran 49:10)*

It is crucial for the mediator to attentively listen to both sides before attempting to resolve the disagreement. Give them uninterrupted time to share their thoughts, feelings, and worries. It's critical to demonstrate compassion and respect for the feelings of all parties. It's critical to pinpoint the areas of disagreement to settle a dispute. Assist your friends in pinpointing the problems that have led to the argument and comprehending the fundamental causes of their disagreements. Mediators must remain neutral and avoid taking sides. Don't judge or place blame on any of the parties. Rather, concentrate on identifying ideas that advance reconciliation and benefit both sides.

Encourage your friends to work together to create a win-win solution rather than forcing one on them. Urge them to collaborate to find potential solutions and compromises that satisfy the demands of both sides. Consider getting outside assistance if you believe you cannot resolve the disagreement amicably or if things get too complicated.

After settling the dispute, it's critical to continue supporting and following up with your friends. Verify their commitment to upholding honest communication and respect for one another in the future. Emphasise the significance of promptly and constructively resolving any new difficulties.

The idea of Sulh, which stands for rapprochement and peacemaking, is one of the cornerstones of Islamic mediation. It is considered a very praiseworthy deed and is firmly established in Islamic jurisprudence. Arriving at a mutually agreeable solution entails bringing disagreeing parties together for discussion, compromise, and negotiation. Sulh is essentially a living example of the forgiveness, compassion, and respect for one another vital to Islam.

Additionally, Islamic mediation promotes the application of "Maqasid al-Shariah" or the higher goals of Islamic law, as a framework for resolving disputes. Along with advancing justice, mercy, and the general welfare, these goals also encompass preserving belief, life, intellect, family, and property. Mediators can make sure that their interventions produce results that are not just morally and ethically just but also legally sound by coordinating their efforts with these overall objectives.

Lastly, Islamic mediation strongly emphasises the value of trust, privacy, and confidentiality in fostering positive relationships between parties. Mediators follow strict norms of conduct and ethical standards to guarantee the efficacy and integrity of the mediation process. By upholding confidentiality and objectivity, mediators can establish a secure environment where parties can work towards resolution and consider innovative solutions without worrying about criticism or retaliation.

Chapter Eight

Friendship with Allah (SWT)

The Concept of Friendship with Allah (SWT)

Faith is greatly influenced by the abundance of good and reliable individuals. Those who have committed themselves to serving God fully and totally in surrender are known as Auliya-Allah (SWT), or the "friends of Allah (SWT)." They are sincere about Allah (SWT), spend their lives purposefully for him, and embody Allah's (SWT) benevolence and compassion.

> *Allah (SWT) says: "Beware, Allah's friends have no fear nor do they grieve. They believe and are mindful of Allah, for them are glad tidings in this worldly life and in the Hereafter" (Quran: 62-64)*

The dangers of this world and the next are not a source of anxiety for the Auliya-Allah (SWT). They also don't lament the loss of anything worthwhile. They don't fear their adversaries because they believe in Allah (SWT). Because they grasp the creation and rely on Allah (SWT), they are free from fear and grief and feel that Divine wisdom is the best. This does not imply that the "friends of Allah (SWT)" won't encounter challenges; rather, it means that "they will be tried." They will, however, rise to the occasion, be patient, resilient, and brave in the face of these hardships and difficult tests.

> *"There are seven whom Allah will shade on a Day when there is no shade but His Shade: (1) a just ruler, (2) a youth who grew up in the worship of Allah, (3) a person whose heart is attached to the mosques, (4) two men who love and meet each other and depart from each other for the sake of Allah, (5) a man who is invited (to sin) by a woman of beauty and position, but he says: 'I fear Allah', (6) a man who gives in charity and conceals it so that his left hand does not know what his right hand has given, and (7) a man who remembers Allah in solitude and his eyes shed tears." (Sahih Bukhari)*

> *Allah (SWT) says in the Quran: "And keep your soul content with those who call on their Lord morning and evening, seeking His face, and let not your eyes pass beyond them, seeking the pomp and glitter of this Life; nor obey any whose heart We have permitted to neglect the remembrance of Us, one who follows his own desires, whose case has gone beyond all bounds." (Quran 18:28)*

Why is Auliya-Allah significant to us?

These individuals lead modest but remarkable lives. They have assumed the duty of establishing Islam's legitimacy in the eyes of the world, which is their gift to Islam. Their existence is a testament to Allah's (SWT) majesty, love, and mercy.

They bear witness to the divine truth as "shaheed." In addition to resisting social evils and adhering to the Prophet's (PBUH) teachings, they exhibit exceptional qualities to promote Islam positively.

Key Aspects of the Spiritual Bond with Allah (SWT)

The relationship with Allah (SWT) is undoubtedly the most important of all the relationships Muslims can have. It regulates every aspect of human interaction in the cosmos. Muslims preserve this essential bond and separate from false bonds when they recognise and cultivate their relationship with Allah (SWT).

They consequently develop into devout servants of their Lord, cherished family members, honest citizens, and kind-hearted people concerned about all people's well-being.

All Muslims must have a close spiritual connection to Allah (SWT). Worshipping Allah (SWT) is a crucial approach since it deepens the connection between a believer and Allah (SWT). Through worship, one can communicate with his Lord.

In Islam, worship has special importance because it demonstrates that a person is a true Muslim when they embrace and carry out the dictates of the Almighty Allah (SWT).

The primary goal of worship is to become closer to Allah (SWT) by doing what He enjoys and finds pleasing. Worship needs to be founded on unambiguous principles and devoid of deviation.

> *The Almighty Allah (SWT) states in the Holy Quran:*
> *"And I did not create the jinn and mankind except to worship me." (Quran 51:56)*

Islam's five pillars, which cover the essential elements of devotion, allow Muslims to strengthen their bond with Allah (SWT).

1 – Testimony of Faith (Shahadah)

The first of the five fundamental tenets is the voluntary and conscious assertion that, "There is nothing worthy of worship except Allah (SWT), and Muhammad (PBUH) is the Messenger of Allah (SWT)."

This assertion, which affirms that no partners can be linked to Allah (SWT) and Muhammad (PBUH) is Allah's (SWT) last prophet, is the cornerstone of Islam. Because of this belief, Muslims look to the teachings of Prophet Muhammad (PBUH) and God's revelation (the Quran) for life direction.

2 – Prayer (Salah)

Muslims must pray five times a day to maintain a spiritual relationship with God and remind themselves of their life's purpose. They work to build a close spiritual bond with their Creator by being sincere, confessing their sins, and praying directly to God throughout the day.

> *"Recite what has been revealed to you of the Book and establish prayer. Indeed, prayer prohibits immorality and wrongdoing, and the remembrance of Allah is greater. And Allah knows that which you do."(Quran 29:45)*

> *"The first deed for which a person will be called to account on the Day of Judgment will be his prayer. If it is good, he will be successful, and if it is bad, he will be a loser." (Sunah Abi Dawud)*

3 – Charity (Zakah)

This yearly donation goes to the impoverished. 2.5% of Muslims' annual savings must be donated to the underprivileged, destitute, and downtrodden. Charity is one of the main pillars of Islamic social welfare, promoting a fair society in which everyone's fundamental needs are met.

> *"Take from their wealth a charity by which you purify them and cause them to increase, and invoke [Allah's blessings] upon them. Indeed, your invocations are reassurance for them. And Allah is Hearing and Knowing."* (Quan 9:103)

4 – Fasting (Sawm)

Muslims abstain from food, liquids, and sexual activity from sunrise to sunset during the ninth month of the Muslim lunar calendar, Ramadan. It's an act of self-discipline and spiritual purification that makes it possible to intentionally suppress negative behaviours as well as to develop empathy for others who are less fortunate. As Muslims overcome their body's basic cravings and their tongue's destructive behaviours, fasting also helps them strengthen their willpower.

> *"The month of Ramadan [is that] in which was revealed the Qur'an, guidance for the people and clear proofs of guidance and criterion. So whoever sights [the new moon of] the month, let him fast it..."(Quran 2:185)*

5 – Pilgrimage (Hajj)

If a Muslim is financially and physically capable, they should make the pilgrimage (travel) to Mecca at least once in their lifetime. Following the customs of Prophet Abraham (AS), Muslims of all races and nationalities come together in equality to worship Allah (SWT), symbolising the unity of humanity.

> *"The reward for an accepted Hajj is nothing less than Paradise." (Sahih Bukhari)*

Conditions of Faith

Believing in Allah (SWT), His angels, His books, His messengers, and the Last Day is one of the basic requirements for being a close friend of Allah (SWT).

> *"Verily, the allies and close friends of Allah will have no fear nor will they grieve those who believe and guard against evil." (Quran 10:62-63)*

Following the teachings of the Holy Prophet (PBUH) is the next condition that needs to be fulfilled to become Allah's (SWT) friend. Allah (SWT) has laid out a lofty premise in the Holy Quran that is certain to lead to the Divine.

> *"Say: If you love Allah then follow me; Allah will love you." (Quran 3:31)*

To communicate Allah's (SWT) directives and prohibitions, as well as His promise and warning, the Prophet (PBUH) acts as a mediator between Allah (SWT) and His creation. Therefore, anyone who thinks that there is any way to reach Allah (SWT) that does not involve obeying Muhammad (PBUH) is one of the Shaytan's close buddies.

Close friendship with Allah (SWT), may only be obtained by adhering to Islamic teachings and living one's life in accordance with them.

Achieving genuine fear of Allah (SWT) and protecting oneself from evil is another crucial requirement for gaining Allah's (SWT) close companionship.

> *"Verily, the allies and close friends of Allah will have no fear nor will they grieve those who believe and guard against evil." (Quran 10:62-63)*

Ibn Zayd (RA) said, 'Those who believe and guard against evil.' According to him, religion is not accepted by Allah (SWT) unless it's accompanied with taqwa, or fear of Allah (SWT) and protection from evil.

> *"The closest of the people to me are those who fear Allah and guard against evil, whoever they are and wherever they are." (Ahmad)*

Furthermore, the creation may develop a close relationship with Allah (SWT) due to various actions. These behaviours include excessively remembering Allah (SWT), adhering to the Sunnah in all areas, spending time with devout people who have a close relationship with Allah (SWT), being grateful for Allah's blessings, being steadfast in upholding Shari'ah laws, and, lastly, generously always asking Allah (SWT) for anything that is needed.

Therefore, to be a believer, we must possess two essential attributes: we must worship Allah (SWT) alone, without forming relationships with Him, and we must adhere to the customs of Prophet Muhammad (PBUH). Furthermore, we require "Taqwa (piety)". "Conscious of Allah (SWT)" is what it signifies. Doing what Allah (SWT) mandates and refraining from doing what is forbidden will put a wall between us and the fire of Allah (SWT). If we are devout believers, we are friends of Allah (SWT), known as Taqwa.

> *The Prophet (PBUH) says that Allah (SWT) says: "Whoever has harmed a friend of mine, I have announced war against him (Al-Bukhari)*

Using Quran to Build a Solid Relationship with Allah (SWT)

The Quran is Allah's (SWT) word! It is His method of speaking to us. The Quran was sent down by him to provide us with instruction. Therefore, having a close relationship with the Quran is crucial.

Muslims learn from studying the Quran that to have a good and proper relationship with Allah (SWT), they must align themselves with His divine qualities. Every attribute of Allah (SWT) requires people to possess particular heart, spirit, and behaviour traits. We ought to develop a strong bond with the Quran, equivalent to a strong bond with Allah (SWT)!

> *"Verily Allah raises nations by this book (the Qur'an) and puts down (i.e. destroys) others by it." (Sahih Muslim)*

Importance of Dhikr and Dua

Dhikr, which means "remembrance or mention" in Arabic, has the plural form, Adhkar. However, in a religious sense, it refers to remembering and mentioning Allah (SWT); it's worship, which is simply praising Allah (SWT) and exalting Him verbally and internally. Phrases like "SubhanAllah," "Alhamdulillah," and "Masha'Allah are a few simple and easy Adhkar.

Each of these phrases has significance, we can repeat them as often as we like and reap the benefits. Engaging in the remembrance of Allah (SWT) (e.g., saying SubhanAllah, Alhamdulillah, Allahu Akbar) keeps the heart connected to Him.

Dua (Supplication) is a direct and intimate conversation between a believer and Allah (SWT), demonstrating dependence and trust in His mercy. It allows believers to express gratitude for blessings, seek guidance in times of uncertainty, and request help for their needs. Dua is an act of worship that strengthens faith and brings spiritual comfort.

> *Allah (SWT) promises to respond to sincere supplications, as mentioned in the Quran: "Call upon Me; I will respond to you" (Qur'an 40:60)*

Thus, Dhikr and dua serve as a means of maintaining the supplicant's relationship with Allah (SWT).

Other Ways to Stay Connected with Allah (SWT)

A believer's relationship with Allah (SWT) is not only based on duty but also on deep love and gratitude. Recognising Allah's (SWT) mercy, blessings, and guidance cultivates a sense of appreciation and strengthens the spiritual connection. Faith in Allah (SWT) means trusting His wisdom, especially during hardships.

Sabr (patience) and Tawakkul (reliance on Allah SWT) help believers navigate challenges with the understanding that Allah's plan is always for their ultimate good.

Human beings are imperfect, and mistakes are inevitable. However, through Tawbah (repentance), believers can renew their bond with Allah (SWT), seeking His forgiveness and striving to improve. Consistent faith, worship, and righteous actions nurture the spiritual bond between believers and Allah (SWT). The goal is to attain closeness to Allah (SWT) in this life and eternal success in the hereafter (Jannah).

Chapter Nine

Friendship Ethics in Islam

Ethical Guidelines for Friendships

Friendship is a valuable relationship that thrives on trust, honesty, and respect. However, negative behaviours drain our energy, weakening this bond and causing misconceptions or conflicts. Managing these undesirable behaviours causes us to feel distressed, which alters us in many ways. It affects us emotionally and makes it difficult for us to trust anymore.

Some friendships endure a lifetime. Others may have situational friendships, existing only at specific stages of a person's life. But regardless of the dynamic you're in, it could be beneficial to refrain from small actions that could jeopardise friendship. Some people might not recognise an underlying issue in a platonic dispute until it's too late. Examining the "little behaviours" that can lead to major relationship closures may be helpful if you're wondering why your friendships don't continue or why a long-term friendship has ended.

Certain obstacles keep coming up, specific routines that we unconsciously participate in. However, these errors can be preventing friendships from blossoming. These actions badly affect both parties involved, but as Muslims we have a lot of support from Islamic teachings that have provided us guidelines to handle all the aspects of our life beautifully. Thus, to build and maintain a strong bond among friends, Islam has provided ethical guidelines for fruitful outcomes. Let's have a look on them in detail:

Avoiding Gossip (Gheebah) and Backbiting (Namimah) among Friends

One of the numerous gifts Allah (SWT) gave us was the ability to speak. Despite being a little organ, the tongue can follow Allah's (SWT) commands, the Prophet's (PBUH) teachings, and the Quran. By doing so, one can receive rewards here on Earth and in the Hereafter. The person who disobeys Allah (SWT) by using his speech, however, does not show gratitude to Allah (SWT) and ultimately destroys himself.

Being grateful to Allah (SWT) undoubtedly entails abstaining from doing what is prohibited with the blessings Allah (SWT) has given us. It is important to understand that tongue sins can range in severity. One should be informed that some of these transgressions result in excommunication from Islam. Gossiping (Gheebah) and Backbiting (Namimah) are tongue sins.

Many of us may gossip, or gheebah, without even realising how dangerous it is. Gheebah is a serious offence in Islam. Because it harms people, spreads negativity, and destroys relationships, the Prophet Muhammad (PBUH) firmly advised against it. Talking negatively about someone when they are not around is known as gheebah. It's still gossip, even if what you're saying is accurate.

The negativity you disseminate can harm other people's perspectives and cause needless resentment, even if the person you're talking about never finds out. Gheebah hurts everyone by sowing the seeds of mistrust, jealousy, and rage. Any healthy connection is built on trust, which is broken when we spread rumours about your friends. If your friends find out you speak behind their backs, they can turn away from you, which can sour relationships with your friends.

> *According to the Prophet (PBUH), gossip (ghibah) is when you say something about your Muslim brother that he finds offensive. "What if that thing I spoke was something true about him?" was the question posed to the Prophet. According to the Prophet, "If it was in him, then you committed the sin of gossip (ghibah), and if it was not in him, therefore you have committed al-buhtan"—a sin that is much more serious than gossip. (Sahih Muslim)*

Similar to this, backbiting, or Namimah, is a malignant disease that affects people's souls. Tongues spread it and cause family ties to be severed and loved ones to be separated. Love and fraternity are hallmarks of Islamic society because smiles decorate faces, and love adorns hearts. Good friendship and fraternity are the cornerstones of relationships.

Anything that incites animosity and hostility among believers is forbidden by Allah (SWT). The term "backbiting" refers to the act of denigrating a believer when they are not present, regardless of whether the supposed weakness was related to his body, ancestry, behaviour, deeds, comments, religion, or life, or any other flaws that are [often] hidden from the public.

Likewise, it makes no difference if the description was verbally or through gesture. Backbiting has been explained by Almighty Allah (SWT) in a way that makes the body and mind dislike it. It's stated:

> *"And some of you should not backbite the others: would anyone of you like to eat the flesh of his dead brother? No, you abhor it." (Quran 49:12)*

> *The Prophet Muhammad (PBUH) said: "Do you know what backbiting is?" They said, "Allah and His Messenger know best." He said, "It is to mention about your brother something he dislikes." (Sahih Muslim)*

And according to the Prophet (PBUH), the penalty is harsh:

> *"When I was taken up to heaven I passed by people who had nails of copper and were scratching their faces and their breasts. I said: 'Who are these people, Gabriel?' He replied: 'They are those who were given to backbiting and who aspersed people's honour.'" (Abu Dawud)*

Thus the Quran frequently warns Muslims about the sins of the mouth by mentioning about these sins in different verses as:

> *"Do not concern yourself with things about which you have no knowledge. Verily, your hearing, sight, and heart — all of them will be called to account" (Quran 17:36)*

> *"Oh you who believe! If a wicked person comes to you with any news, ascertain the truth, lest you harm people unwittingly, and afterwards become full of repentance for what you have done (Quran 49:6)*

> *"Why do not the believing men and women, whenever such [a rumour] is heard, think the best of one another*

> *and say, "This is an obvious falsehood"? ... When you take it up with your tongues, uttering with your mouths something of which you have no knowledge, you deem it a light matter whereas in the sight of God it is an awful thing!" (Quran 24:12-15)*

Therefore, faith exhorts us to see the best in ourselves and others. A believer treats others with honour and dignity. Spreading rumours, gossip, or backbiting someone else is not acceptable for a Muslim.

Upholding Trustworthiness (Amanah) and Honesty in Relationships

Trustworthiness, or Amanah, is the cornerstone of strong friendships. Muslims are encouraged to keep their friends' trust and confide in them regarding important matters by being dependable and trustworthy in their social relationships.

The word "amanah" means trust. One of Allah's (SWT) lovely names, "Mu'min," is the collective term for those who believe in Him. It signifies that He is the source of security, that He gives his servants faith, and that He is the one who establishes their reliability. Additionally, He is the one who has made His prophets trustworthy and bestowed upon them the quality of "trust."

Accordingly, the "mu'min" is the person who possesses iman, or faith, has been trusted, inspires trust, and is trustworthy. One of the core tenets of social and personal life interactions is being reliable and honouring commitments, or being faithful to one's word. People must be trustworthy and honour their commitments.

Amanah is the moral obligation to carry out one's duties suitably. It plays a significant role in a Muslim's life. Allah (SWT) gave us clear instructions on how to do Amanah correctly.

> *Allah (SWT) says: "Surely Allah commands you to make over trusts to their owners and that when you judge between people you judge with justice; surely Allah admonishes you with what is excellent; surely Allah is Seeing, Hearing." (Quran 4:58)*

Amanah includes keeping one's secrets as well.

> *Holy Prophet (PBUH) said: "If a man says something then turns away, it becomes a trust [which should not be disclosed by the one who heard it." (Abu Dawud)*

Amanah, also known as one of the traits of the Prophet Muhammad (PBUH), is called trustworthy, which is defined as accountability, honesty, and dependability. In relationships between individuals, groups, and states, a trustworthy (amanah) serves as a strong basis. Relationships cannot be trusted without trustworthy (amanah) actions.

When Amanah is fulfilled, one's social and personal lives gain significance. A sincere believer possesses the attribute of fulfilling Amanah, while a hypocrite, or Munafiq, violates it. Another Hadith states that a person who does not satisfy Amanah lacks faith and religion.

> *As narrated by Anas (RA) the Holy Prophet (PBUH) said: "There is no faith for the one who has no trust, and there is no religion for the one that does not fulfil his promises." (Musnad Ahmad). As narrated by Abu Huriarah (RA), the Mesenger of Allah (PBUH) said: "Signs of a hypocrite are three: whenever he speaks he lies; whenever he promises, he breaks his promises; and whenever he is entrusted with an Amanah, he betrays his trust (Amanah); even if he fasts and prays and even if he claims he is a Muslim." (Sahih Bukhari)*

At the same time, honesty is the foundation of any wholesome and significant relationship, particularly friendships. Sharing the truth about yourself and your life can help you and your friends become closer. Speaking the truth without altering it is the definition of honesty. It means that all of your actions should be consistent with all of your words. In the fight against the world's falsehoods, Muslims view honesty and truthfulness as their weapons.

Good manners are a hallmark of Islam, and believers should spread these virtues to one another. Before becoming a prophet, Prophet Muhammad (PBUH) was said to be honest and truthful. Thus, honesty is one of the most essential qualities a person should possess to build a strong foundation for friendship.

Prophet Muhammad (PBUH) has a lovely statement emphasising the truth:

> *"I enjoin you to be truthful, for truthfulness leads to righteousness and righteousness leads to Paradise. A man may continue to tell the truth and endeavor to be truthful until he is recorded with Allah as a speaker of truth. And beware of lying, for lying leads to wickedness and wickedness leads to Hell. A man may continue to tell lies and endeavor to tell lies until he is recorded with Allah as a liar." (Sahih Muslim)*

Islam exhorts followers to be truthful with their Lord, themselves, and the community. Being true to oneself encourages self-accountability, which is necessary for acknowledging, accepting, and making amends for one's shortcomings. To become honest with Allah (SWT), one must worship Him with sincerity and persistently obey His precepts. The Holy Quran states that the righteous will be respected and shielded from bad luck on the Day of Judgement.

> *"Allah will declare: "This is the Day when 'only' the faithful will benefit from their faithfulness. Theirs are Gardens under which rivers flow, to stay there forever and ever. Allah is pleased with them and they are pleased with Him. That is the ultimate triumph (Quran 5:119)*

The sincerity of one's actions and behaviours is another aspect of honesty. A person will act honourably and morally in every facet of life, avoiding all forms of dishonesty, if they are truthful with Allah (SWT) and themselves. Fundamentally, dishonesty arises from a lack of integrity and a departure from the path of righteousness. Those who choose to speak the truth rather than lie are cherished by Allah (SWT).

In the short term, lying may appear simple, but in the long run, telling the truth is a far easier choice that brings individuals peace of mind. People should remember to embrace honesty, as Allah (SWT) will love and reward those who do so, both in this life and the next.

Respecting Differences and Diversity

Diversity encompasses more than just distinctions in race or ethnicity; it also includes variances in background, age, gender, sexual orientation, and personal philosophy. However, by accepting differences and being willing to explore them, people can find that these differences can enhance their own lives and possibly indicate ways to improve or simplify them, or that it may be beneficial to approach things in new and different ways.

Building a more welcoming and peaceful society requires respecting individual differences. It entails appreciating and accepting people for who they are, their distinct histories, experiences, and viewpoints. Let's have a look at how diversity plays a role in friendships;

Embracing Cultural and Religious Diversity

Having friends from diverse backgrounds, such as different races, ages, genders, socioeconomic levels, and cultural customs, is known as diversity in friendships. This diversity enhances interpersonal relationships and increases understanding by bringing distinct viewpoints and life experiences into one's social group.

Challenge is necessary for the development of any healthy friendship. Friends can learn more about one another and the world at large when they are exposed to ideas and perspectives that differ from their own. This is even truer when you have friends from a wider range of backgrounds.

It's likely that you'll all bring various perspectives to the table and challenge one another with them, fostering interpersonal growth both within and outside of these relationships, when you surround yourself with individuals who are very different from you.

Islam is a religion that unites people from all walks of life through the shared belief in the unity of Allah (God), transcending continents and cultures. This large population has a stunning tapestry of various traditions, languages, and rituals. As Muslims, we must acknowledge and appreciate this variety while creating a welcoming atmosphere where everyone is treated with respect and worth.

The life of the Holy Prophet introduced Islam to the Arabian people, and the Holy Prophet (PBUH) changed the community by working to establish equality and social justice. Eliminating racism and prejudice during the Holy Prophet's (PBUH) lifetime was one of the most significant social reforms he brought about in a society that was extremely repressive and hostile to anyone who was not their own. The Prophet (PBUH) made a concerted effort to restrain the racist tendencies of the people to establish an equitable system.

The Prophet (PBUH) said, "There is no superiority of an Arab over a non-Arab, or of non-Arab over an Arab, and superiority of neither a white man over a black man nor a black man over a white man except by virtue of piety." (Musnad Ahmad)

The life of the Holy Prophet (PBH) himself exemplifies racial equality in Islam, and some of his closest companions were from around the globe. A Persian man named Salman al-Muhammadi constantly sought solutions related to heavenly knowledge. After meeting the Holy Prophet (PBUH) he accepted Islam because he sought a faith that valued humility, kindness, and charity. He travelled to Medina after years of adversity, where he encountered the Holy Prophet (PBUH) and converted to Islam. He became one of the Holy Prophet's (PBUH) closest and most devoted associates.

An Ethiopian slave named Bilal the Muezzin (Muadhin) resided in the Arabian Peninsula. Despite being severely tortured by his owners due to his faith, he was among the first people to accept Islam after the Holy Prophet (PBUH) declared his prophetic status. He became one of the most well-known companions of the Messenger (PBUH) because of his earnest declaration of loyalty to Allah (SWT) and submission to the Prophet (PBUH).

According to Islamic teachings, regardless of their country or clan, people who are aware of God and demonstrate that awareness in their behaviour are the most esteemed in God's eyes.

As Allah (SWT) mentions in the Quran, "We have created you all male and female and have made you nations and tribes so that you would recognise each other. The most honourable among you in the sight of God is the most pious of you. God is All-knowing and All-aware." (Quran 31:18)

Chapter Ten

Stories of Friendship from Islamic History

Inspirational Stories of Friendship

Numerous instances of strong, enduring friendships that have provided believers with direction and inspiration may be found throughout Islamic history. Sahaba's life is replete with morals and stories that illustrate Islamic principles and how one might apply them to their own life, especially in their friendships. To promote and cultivate Islamic principles, a few of the Sahabah's stories are included below, along with a few instances from their fortunate lives.

The word "sahabi" in Arabic literally means "friend" or "companion." Someone who saw Prophet Muhammad (PBUH), accepted him, acted along with him, and maintained his belief until the time of his death" is what the term signifies in the religious context. One can use either "sahaba" or "ashab" for the plural.

Although companions enjoy unparalleled grandeur and a high rank, we must acknowledge that these attributes were not bestowed upon them as an unmerited favour. From the moment they decided to become Muslims, they had a strong bond with the Prophet (PBUH) and complied with the precepts of their new faith with humility. They spent most of their lives with the Prophet (PBUH), followed his counsel and judgement, and made significant sacrifices alongside him for the advancement and propagation of Islam, even though they converted to Islam at various times. The stories of these companions of Holy Prophet (PBUH) serve as a beacon of light. Let's explore them in detail!

Examples of Companionship and Loyalty from Islamic history

Hazrat Abu Bakr (RA)

The Prophet Muhammad's closest friend was Abu Bakr. The Prophet (PBUH) used to talk about Abu Bakr and say that he was the only one who, after learning about Islam, never hesitated to adopt it. Abu Bakr (RA) supported the Prophet (PBUH) no matter what. In the early days of Islam, his steadfast support was crucial.

Abu Bakr (RA) was renowned for his honesty and integrity even before he converted to Islam. He was a prosperous businessman known for his honest transactions. Even in the pre-Islamic world, which was frequently characterised by corruption and dishonesty, he was a man of great morals and ideals. Because of these qualities, he was well-liked in Makkah.

For the Prophet (PBUH), Abu Bakr (RA) was not just a friend but also a reliable counsellor and a pillar of support. Abu Bakr (RA) supported the Prophet (PBUH) when things got tough. Abu Bakr (RA) supported the Prophet (PBUH) and his adherents when the Quraysh elders in Makkah turned against them. Despite being persecuted alongside Muslims, he never abandoned the Prophet (PBUH).

> *They were faithful to each other and loved each other. The Prophet (PBUH) said: "If I were to take a close friend, I would have taken Abu Bakr (RA) as my friend, but he is my brother and companion."(Sahih Muslim)*

Muslims respect Hazrat Abu Bakr (RA) for his loyalty and dependability. Strong support or loyalty to someone or something is the definition of loyalty. By supporting Prophet Muhammad (PBUH), he demonstrated his devotion to him.

The Prophet Muhammad (PBUH) was steadfastly supported by Abu Bakr (RA) throughout the "Battle of Badr," the first significant conflict with the Quraysh. Abu Bakr (RA) fought bravely on the frontlines, supported the Muslim warriors physically and morally, and raised their spirits, all of which helped them win. Like the Muslim defeat in the Battle of Uhud, Abu Bakr (RA) stood his ground and protected the Prophet (PBUH) amid the mayhem. Even when he had to deal with personal difficulties, like his son fighting for the Quraysh, his bravery and devotion were clear throughout the conflict.

Abu Bakr's credibility was truly tested after the Prophet's (PBUH) passing when he was faced with a challenging circumstance. Abu Bakr (RA) was charged with maintaining the integrity of the Muslim Empire and bringing the many Arab tribes back together after they wanted to break away. He worked diligently to accomplish this goal, proving his reliability, and successfully reintegrating the Arab tribes.

Ali bin Abi Talib (RA)

Ali ibn Talib (RA) is a prominent figure in Islam and a role model for Muslims. His life and deeds inspire people worldwide, both Muslims and non-Muslims. In Islam, Ali (RA) is one of the ten honoured companions who will enter Jannah in the Hereafter, as determined by Allah (SWT).

When he was ten years old, Ali bin Abi Talib became the first young person to convert to Islam. After observing the Prophet (PBUH) and Hazrat Khadijah (RA) praying, 'Ali (RA) asked them what they were doing and later converted to Islam, initially keeping his conversion a secret.

Even in his early years, his iron bravery and courage were evident. For instance, Ali (RA) stayed behind and slept in the Prophet's (PBUH) bed on the night when the Prophet (PBUH) and Abu Bakr (RA) had to depart for Mecca during the migration from Mecca to Medina. The Prophet (PBUH) also assigned him the responsibility of returning some of the people's possessions under his care.

Ali (RA) was so bold and devoted to the Prophet (PBUH) that he took on the mission without hesitation and risked his life. He had an unrivalled devotion to the Prophet (PBUH). He dedicated his life to Allah (SWT) and Prophet (PBUH) teachings, living according to the precepts established by the Prophet (PBUH).

Zubair al-'Awwam bin (RA)

Zubair bin al-'Awwam (RA), known for his courage, was one of the first seven people to convert to Islam. Zubair (RA) was raised with perseverance and discipline, and his devotion to the Prophet (PBUH) led to him being referred to as "Hawari Rasulillah" (the Prophet's PBUH devoted disciple). Both his academic pursuits and his military leadership, which included his crucial part in the Battle of Uhud, demonstrated his dedication. Even though Zubair died in the midst of political strife, his legacy is still admirable.

Mush'ab bin 'Umair (RA)

Known for his intelligence and charm, Mush'ab bin 'Umair (RA) became an Islamist during the covert preaching at Dar al-Arqam. He persevered in the face of strong family opposition, including material and physical difficulties. Mush'ab (RA) had a crucial role at Medina since he was responsible for teaching the Ansar about Islam, which resulted in many conversions. His commitment continued on the battlefield, when he was martyred after carrying the Muslim banner throughout the Battle of Uhud.

These Companions of the Prophet (PBUH) made significant contributions to the spread of Islam worldwide. Their varied personalities, unshakeable dedication, and readiness to make sacrifices for their convictions serve as powerful examples for future generations.

Narratives of Friendship Among the Early Muslims and Scholars

Among the early Muslims, one of the most touching examples of brotherhood was between Salman Al-Farsi and Abu Darda. When the Prophet (PBUH) paired the Muhajirun (emigrants from Makkah) with the Ansar (helpers from Madinah), Abu Darda welcomed Salman into his home. Salman advised Abu Darda on moderation in worship and self-care, showing that true friendship involves guiding one another toward balance in life. The Prophet later affirmed Salman's wisdom, highlighting that a sincere friend looks out for their companion's well-being.

Another touching story is that of Mus'ab ibn Umair and Sa'd ibn Abi Waqqas. Mus'ab, a wealthy young man who had given up luxury for Islam, was instrumental in spreading the message in Madinah. Sa'd, an early convert, supported Mus'ab in his mission, providing companionship and security. Their friendship was centered on faith and sacrifice, demonstrating how true companionship transcends material wealth.

The Sacrifices of the Sahabahs for Islam

The devoted adherents of the Prophet Muhammad (PBUH) were ardent Muslims. Throughout history, classical scholars have praised their stories of bravery, grandeur, suffering, and victory. Since their sacrifices will undoubtedly motivate us to be better Muslims with better Iman and Taqwa, we should all learn from them.

Many of the Prophet Muhammad's (PBUH) companions were traders who exemplified honesty and integrity throughout that time. Abdur-Rahman ibn Awf (RA), renowned for his financial savvy, was one of them. He requested the location of the marketplace instead of financial aid after moving to Medina. He achieved success via hard work and moral behaviour, proving that money can be used for social good and charity when it's obtained in a moral manner.

Before converting to Islam, Uthman ibn Affan (RA), another renowned friend, was a prosperous trader. He used his wealth to help Muslim society; for example, he bought the Ruma Well so that the Medina residents would have free water. His generosity went even beyond, funding important public welfare initiatives and military campaigns.

Abu Bakr As-Siddiq (RA), another outstanding individual, was a successful businessman whose fortune was vital to the early development of Islam. He demonstrated that material prosperity and spiritual fervour could coexist peacefully by using his wealth to assist the Prophet's (PBUH) mission and free slaves.

In the same vein, Sa'd ibn Abi Waqqas (RA) traded while still having a strong religious conviction. He was able to promote Islam and give back to the society because of the revenues from his business. His strict financial principles established a standard for striking a balance between religion and business.

These friends were outstanding examples of how honest and equitable trading may promote both individual wealth and the common good. Their lives continue to serve as a model for moral business practices, showing how religiously motivated commercial success may advance society and lead to spiritual fulfilment.

Friendship Guidelines from the Quran

Friends have a vital and significant role in a person's life since they greatly influence the decisions that person makes. For this reason, Islam also discusses friendship. Islam strongly emphasises choosing the proper friends because it recognises the value of friendships in a person's life. That's why the Quran has given us precise rules regarding friendship, let's discuss them:

As Muslims, we believe we all have the noble quality of friendship with Allah (SWT). He obviously considers us to be buddies, and he has close friends among people. In the Quran Allah (SWT) states:

> *"And who is better in religion than one who submits himself to Allah while being a doer of good and follows the religion of Abraham, inclining toward truth? And Allah took Abraham as an intimate friend." (Quran 4:125)*

> *"For them will be the Home of Peace with their Lord. And He will be their protecting friend because of what they used to do." (Quran 6:127)*

Righteousness is the foundation of true friendship. Allah (SWT) says in the Quran:

> *"And not equal are the good deed and the bad. Repel [evil] by that [deed] which is better; and thereupon the one whom between you and him is enmity [will become] as though he was a devoted friend." (Quran 41:34)*

> *"Close friends, that Day, will be enemies to each other, except for the righteous." (Quran 43:67)*

Our acceptance of dishonesty is a prerequisite for false friendship. Quran has mentioned it as:

> "And indeed, they were about to tempt you away from that which We revealed to you in order to [make] you invent about Us something else; and then they would have taken you as a friend." (Quran 17:73)

Taking His adversaries as friends is forbidden by Allah (SWT). This does not imply that we should avoid talking to unbelievers genuinely seeking the truth.

> "O you who have believed, do not take My enemies and your enemies as allies, extending to them affection while they have disbelieved in what came to you of the truth, having driven out the Prophet and yourselves [only] because you believe in Allah, your Lord. If you have come out for jihad in my cause and seeking means to My approval, [take them not as friends]. You confide to them affection, but I am most of what you have concealed and what you have declared. And whoever does it among you has certainly strayed from the soundness of the way." (Quran 60:1)

Islam places a great value on friendship, which influences a person's decisions and character. The Quran emphasises that genuine friendship is founded on kindness and faith and offers explicit instructions on choosing moral partners. As demonstrated by His intimate relationship with Prophet Abraham (AS), Allah (SWT) is the believers' best friend and protector.

False friendships based on dishonesty lead one astray, yet sincere friendships encourage and support one another. Thus, Islam encourages believers to seek sincere companionship that aligns with righteousness and truth.

Chapter Eleven

Applying Lessons of Friendship in Everyday Life

Friendship is one of the most profound aspects of human existence, shaping our experiences and guiding our moral compass. In Islam, friendships are not just about social interactions but are deeply embedded in faith, righteousness, and the pursuit of goodness.

Let's explore how we can apply the lessons of friendship learned from Islamic teachings in our daily lives, ensuring that our relationships align with the values of sincerity, loyalty, and spiritual fulfillment.

Summary of Key Lessons on Friendship in Islam

Islamic teachings emphasise that true friendships are based on mutual love for the sake of Allah (SWT), honesty, trust, and support. Throughout this book, we've examined the various aspects of Islamic friendship, including the examples set by the Prophet Muhammad (PBUH) and his companions.

We've also explored the ethical and moral guidelines provided by the Quran and Hadith regarding selecting and maintaining friendships.

Some of the most important lessons include:

- Choosing friends who remind us of Allah (SWT) and encourage us to act in righteousness.
- Avoiding friendships that lead us away from faith and into sinful behaviour.
- Practising patience, forgiveness, and humility in maintaining strong bonds with our friends.
- Supporting our friends in times of hardship, both emotionally and spiritually.
- Understanding that loyalty (Wafa) in friendship is a reflection of true faith.

Al-Ghazali on the Benefits of Friendship

One of the most well-known Eastern thinkers, Muhammad Ghazali, left behind a rich spiritual legacy. Al-Ghazali studied a wide range of scientific topics, including ethics. He beautifully discussed the advantages of friendship. Al-Ghazali suggests that you should befriend people who behave and speak well and that wise people deserve discourse and friendship.

Befriending the impoverished and those with wounded hearts is essential. Friends talk to each other in social situations, while travelling, or while studying. Friendships will be stronger as they go through difficult times together.

According to Al-Ghazali, everyone needs friends to survive. However, not everyone deserves friendship and discourse, particularly those who struggle with emotional regulation. A person must first be tested before being a friend; if he shares secrets and weaknesses, he isn't suitable for friendship and will likely generate problems and accuse the other person of being a villain.

Al-Ghazali lists five types of people who are unworthy of friendship: those who are ignorant and whose ignorance affects others; those who want good but do the opposite and do not distinguish between good and evil; those who are contentious and lean towards evil; those who are dishonest and take pride in their lies; those who are heartbreaking and may get into trouble; and those who are deprived and capable of cheating in any situation.

Strengthening Existing and Cultivating New Friendships

One way to choose the right friends is by observing their character. Do they engage in good deeds? Do they encourage others to be better? Are they truthful and trustworthy? Surrounding oneself with friends who uplift and inspire is essential for spiritual growth.

Friendships require effort and sincerity. Small acts of kindness, such as checking in on a friend, offering support in difficult times, and simply being there when needed, go a long way in strengthening bonds. The Prophet Muhammad (PBUH) set an excellent example by always treating his companions with kindness and respect.

Active communication is another key component.

> *"When the Prophet would turn to speak to someone, he would turn his whole body towards them and give them his full attention" (Abu Dawud)*

This Hadith teaches us the importance of giving our friends our undivided attention and listening to them with sincerity and empathy.

Disagreements are a natural part of any relationship. However, Islam provides clear guidelines on resolving conflicts peacefully.

> *"And reconcile your mutual differences" (Quran 8:1)*

Whenever conflicts arise, it's important to address them with patience and understanding. Active listening, empathy, and forgiveness are essential. If needed, mediation through a trusted third party, such as an elder or religious leader, can help find a fair resolution.

A true friend is someone who supports and motivates others toward goodness. Strengthening friendships involves encouraging our friends to improve spiritually, reminding them of their religious duties, and standing by them in moments of weakness. We should be friends who inspire others to be better Muslims.

Trust is a cornerstone of friendship. If a friend shares something in confidence, it should be kept private.

> *"When a man tells you something and then looks around, it is a trust." (Tirmidhi)*

Betraying a friend's trust can lead to irreparable damage to the relationship. Upholding honesty and integrity ensures that friendships remain strong and meaningful.

Life is ever-changing, and sometimes, friendships can be tested by distance, shifting priorities, or new responsibilities. However, true friendships endure these challenges. One way to maintain friendships is to actively try to stay in touch. In today's digital age, a simple message or call can keep a connection alive.

Moreover, accepting and adapting to changes with understanding can prevent friendships from fading. If a friend becomes busy with family or work, we should be supportive rather than resentful.

Commitment to Upholding Islamic Values in Friendships

Loyalty and Dependability: Loyalty is one of the most important qualities in friendship. Islam teaches us to stand by our friends in good and bad times. The Prophet (PBUH) demonstrated unwavering loyalty to his companions, especially Abu Bakr (RA), who remained by his side during the most challenging times.

Avoiding Negative Friendships: Just as good friends uplift us, bad friends can lead us astray.

> *"And indeed, they were about to tempt you away from that which We revealed to you." (Quran 17:73)*

It is important to distance ourselves from friendships that promote dishonesty, gossip, and sinful behaviour. Instead, we should seek companionship that brings us closer to righteousness.

Spreading Positivity and Goodness: Friendships should be a source of positivity and encouragement. Islam encourages spreading kindness through words and actions. The Prophet (PBUH) said:

> *"Every good is charity. Indeed, among the good is to meet your brother with a smiling face." (Tirmidhi)*

By being kind, forgiving, and supportive, we can nurture meaningful friendships that benefit us both in this life and the Hereafter.

Friendship is more than just companionship; it's a means to attain Allah's (SWT) pleasure and support one another in life's journey. Islam provides a comprehensive framework for building and maintaining meaningful relationships. By choosing the right friends, upholding trust, resolving conflicts with wisdom, and being a source of encouragement, we can create friendships that benefit us in this world and the Hereafter.

As we conclude this chapter, let's sincerely try to embody Islamic values in our friendships. Let's strive to be friends who bring positivity, guidance, and unwavering support to those around us. May Allah (SWT) bless us with sincere and righteous friends who will be with us in this life and reunite with us in Jannah. Ameen.

Chapter Twelve

Conclusion

Throughout life's journey, caring friends, acquaintances, and companions can bring comfort and support through all its stages. These heartfelt connections become even more precious when we face tough times, offering solace and companionship. When friends are sincere and virtuous, they embody a wonderful character that reflects kindness, excellent behaviour, and uplifting conduct, all of which are gifts from Allah (SWT).

Without question, affection, kindness, and comfort are the results of good behaviour, and the better one behaves, the sweeter and tastier the fruit gets. Friendship is a loving bond between individuals that unites them in every way. The synchronicity of people's natures leads to friendship, which is a reflection of their love. Friendship is built on a foundation of morals.

Islamic teachings emphasise that a true friend is someone who reminds us of Allah (SWT), encourages us to do good, and supports us in times of need. The Prophet Muhammad (PBUH) perfectly exemplified sincere and meaningful friendships. His bond with Abu Bakr (RA) is a timeless lesson in loyalty, trust, and unwavering faith. This level of companionship teaches us that the best friendships are those rooted in love for the sake of Allah (SWT) and guided by sincerity, honesty, and kindness.

Throughout this book, we've explored the significance of friendship (Suhbah) in Islamic teachings, emphasising the importance of surrounding ourselves with righteous company (Suhbah Salihah). Good companionship influences our character and aids us in remaining on the path of righteousness, whilst poor friendships can lead us astray. Islam encourages us to seek friends who draw us closer to our faith and uplift our spirits, rather than those who distract us from our purpose.

No relationship is free from difficulties, and friendships are no exception. Differences in opinions, misunderstandings, and conflicts can arise even between the best of friends. However, Islam provides clear guidance on handling such challenges with wisdom, patience, and forgiveness. The principles of mutual respect, empathy, and open communication are key to resolving conflicts and maintaining strong bonds. When disputes occur, we must seek resolution through kindness and sincerity rather than harbouring resentment or severing ties hastily.

One of our most profound lessons is the importance of loyalty (Wafa) in friendships. A true friend is present during times of happiness and stands by us in moments of hardship. Islam teaches us that supporting our friends emotionally, spiritually, and even financially when needed strengthens our bonds and earns us immense rewards in the sight of Allah (SWT).

As we part ways with this book, let's make a commitment to seek and nurture friendships that align with Islamic values. Let's be mindful of the company we keep, ensuring that our friendships are based on love for Allah (SWT) rather than superficial or materialistic interests. Let's strive to be the kind of friend who uplifts, inspires, and supports others in their journey toward righteousness. May Allah (SWT) grant us sincere and righteous friends who will be with us in this world and reunite with us in Jannah. Ameen.

Find Out More

Website: www.barakahinbusiness.com

Socials: @barakahinbusiness

If you enjoyed this book, kindly leave a review to help expand our reach so others may benefit also.